W0115288

The Dime Novel Western

The Dime Novel Western

Daryl Jones

The Popular Press
Bowling Green State University
Bowling Green, Ohio

The photographs of dime novel covers used to illustrate this volume are from the Collections of the Michigan State University Libraries.

CONTENTS

ORIGIN AND CONTEXT

The thirst for works of the imagination is as strong and universal at the present time as at any former period; and we trust that of the floods which annually pour in upon the reading world, there are some fountains at which the soul may drink and feel itself refreshed and invigorated.

--The Western Monthly Magazine, 1833

Perhaps it was in part the note of confidence sounded in this opening statement of Isaac Appleton Jewett's "Themes for Western Fiction" that won him, in December 1833, the first annual prize for the best essay to appear in the pages of *The Western Monthly Magazine*.[1] Addressed to the writers of America, Jewett's essay made an impassioned plea for a new and distinctly national literature which would draw its subject matter from the rich artistic resources offered by the wilderness West. Citing the wealth of material available to writers in the landscape, characters, and incidents of the frontier, Jewett predicted that it would be from those works of the imagination which distilled the emotional impact of the West that the soul would someday drink and feel refreshed.

Though eloquently phrased, Jewett's call for a national literature nurtured on the frontier experience was not so much a new and original proposal as it was the reflection of a trend well advanced in American letters. Already, at least two epic poems, Daniel Bryan's *The Mountain Muse* (1813) and James Kirk Paulding's *The Backwoodsman* (1818), had heralded the opening of the West; *The Pioneers* (1823), *The Last of the Mohicans* (1826), and *The Prairie* (1827) had won Cooper a prominent place in American literature; and numerous short stories, novels, and pioneer biographies had emerged from the pens of Gilbert Imlay, Hugh Henry Brackenridge, Charles Brockden Brown, James McHenry, N.M. Hentz, William Joseph Snelling, Timothy Flint, Matthew St. Clair Clarke, and James Hall. The late thirties, forties, and fifties spawned an even greater body of literature that utilized frontier settings and incidents. Skilled writers like Cooper, Paulding, and Hall continued to produce Western fiction, and soon they found themselves joined by a coterie of talented newcomers, most notably Robert Montgomery Bird, whose *Nick of the Woods* (1837) won instant acclaim, and William Gilmore Simms, who dramatized life on the Southern Border both in *The Yemassee* (1835) and in the series of works known collectively as the *Border Romances* (1834-1840).

During this same period a number of less talented writers—James Strange French,

Nathaniel B. Tucker, Charles W. Webber, Charles Fenno Hoffman, Emerson Bennett, A.W. Arrington, John Esten Cooke, and Mayne Reid–ground out Western fiction that proved immensely popular. Emerson Bennett's *The Prairie Flower* (1849) and *Leni-Leoti* (1849) sold one hundred thousand copies each, and Bennett's rivals were nearly as successful. Yet with the possible exception of an occasional work by Mayne Reid, these popular novels were poorly written, highly melodramatic, and embarrassingly derivative. John Myers, the hero of Cooke's *Leatherstocking and Silk* (1854), for instance, is an unintentionally amusing replica of Natty Bumppo who, in even the most extreme circumstances, seems incapable of saying anything more profound than "Anan?"[2] By the late 1850s such novels were the rule rather than the exception. Indeed, to such an extent had Western fiction degenerated by 1858 that in June of that year William T. Coggeshall, then the Ohio State Librarian, told the Beta Theta Pi fraternity of Ohio University that "Tomahawks and wigwams, sharp-shooting and hard fights, log cabins, rough speech, dare-devil boldness, bear-hunting and corn-husking, prairie flowers, bandits, lynch-law and no-law-at-all miscellaneously mixed into 25 cents novels...represent the popular idea of Western Literature."[3]

One result of this sudden deterioration in the quality of literature concerning the West has been that interpreters of the early Western have concentrated their efforts almost exclusively on works produced before 1860–particularly those by Cooper, Simms, and Bird. For the same reason, interpreters who credit Wister's *The Virginian* with resurrecting the Western from the murky realm of sub-literature have dealt exclusively with works penned after 1902–those by Andy Adams, Eugene Manlove Rhodes, William McLeod Raine, Emerson Hough, Zane Grey, Frederick Faust, and a host of more recent writers in the six-gun and sagebrush school. Consequently, with regard to the Western, the period between 1860 and 1900 might justly be termed "the forgotten era." Critics of the Western have, of course, concerned themselves with selected works by such writers as Mark Twain, Bret Harte, Hamlin Garland, and Stephen Crane--even though it remains a moot point as to whether or not the works in question are in fact "Westerns." Yet these same critics largely ignore the development during this period of that variety of story which, indisputably, is a Western.[4]

At least two factors account for this critical neglect. On the one hand, almost all Westerns written between 1860 and 1902 appeared as dime novels or story papers printed on cheap pulp paper— a notoriously ephemeral medium. Thus, only a relatively small number of dime novels survive today, and the majority of these are inaccessible to scholars; they are either in the hands of private collectors, or they are crumbling, uncatalogued and unmicrofilmed, in the rare book vaults of a few major libraries. On the other hand, critics have, with some justification, neglected dime novel Westerns because of the genre's undeniable mediocrity. Nevertheless, it was the dime novelist—working in the comparative anonymity of a large publishing house, meeting rigid deadlines, and looking to sales as the sole measure of his artistry— who gradually, over a period of more than fifty years, fashioned many of the Western's most characteristic elements.

As a medium for the dissemination of popular fiction, the dime novel was not a strikingly original development but rather the culmination of a trend in publishing that began in the 1830s. Although the population of the United States was at that time approaching twenty million people, most of whom were literate, the majority of readers were denied access to popular literature by the high cost of hardbound books, and the limited number of libraries. All of this changed with the introduction of the steam rotary press—which lowered printing costs—and the subsequent development of new techniques in marketing and mass distribution. As early as 1839, inspired innovators in the field of publishing began tapping the potential of the mass audience; Wilson & Company of Boston initiated the publication of the weekly story paper with *Brother Jonathan,* a compilation of several short stories and chapters from serial novels, printed on cheap paper, organized in newspaper format, and issued at minimal cost to both publisher and reader. The experiment was an instant success. Other firms, spurred by the example of *Brother Jonathan,* printed their own versions, and succeeding years saw the rise of such popular story papers as *The Flag of Our Union, The New York Ledger, The New York Weekly,* and *The Youth's Companion.*

Although popular fiction in the form of fifteen- and twenty-cent serial novelettes appeared throughout the forties and fifties--series like Ballou's *The Weekly Novelette* or *Gleason's Literary Companion*--the dime novel *per se* did not appear until Erastus and Irwin Beadle, heartened by their initial success with a pamphlet entitled *The Dime Song Book,* conceived the idea of printing entire novels complete under one cover, to be sold for a dime. Engaging the services of a business associate named Robert Adams, and moving from Buffalo to New York City in 1858, they formed the publishing firm which later came to be known as the House of Beadle and Adams. In June 1860 they released the first dime novel: *Malaeska: The Indian Wife of the White Hunter.* Written by an established domestic novelist, Mrs. Ann S. Stephens, this tale of white hunters and noble savages sold 65,000 copies within a few months—a reception that virtually assured the success of the Beadle venture.[5]

The popularity enjoyed by Beadle and Adams' "yellow-back novels" soon attracted other firms into the field. Over the years, the House of Beadle and Adams encountered its stiffest competition from five rivals. In 1863, one of the Beadle printers, George Munro, set out on his own and promptly launched a lucrative series called Munro's Ten Cent Novels. In 1867, Robert De Witt expanded his small publishing house and released the first of 1,118 dime novels that he was to publish in the next ten years. And in 1870, Norman Munro, George's brother, entered the field. Still, the greatest success fell to two relative latecomers, Frank Tousey and Street & Smith. Together with a host of smaller competitors, these firms–based in New York City and aiming their stories at a predominantly eastern audience–dominated the market until the early decades of the twentieth century, when the combined effects of rising second-class postal rates and the burgeoning film industry precipitated the decline of the dime novel.

Though classified under the rubric "dime novel," pulp thrillers released by these firms actually varied widely in format. Some, like *The New York Weekly,* were simply story papers; save for their sensational, black and white woodcut illustrations, they resembled an ordinary newspaper. Others, particularly those that flourished from 1860 to 1888, were issued semi-monthly as seven by five inch pamphlets averaging one hundred pages and priced at a dime. After 1888, publishers enlarged the format to twelve by eight inches in an effort to accommodate larger illustrations on the front cover; dime novels of this period ran from sixteen to thirty-two pages in length, and sold for only a nickel. In the 1890s these so-called "nickel weeklies" began to appear with color illustrations, and shortly thereafter some stories assumed the format of the modern paperback novel. Publishers were not, however, reluctant to release a story in more than one format, or even to reprint the same story several times under different titles. If a tale serialized in a weekly story paper received a favorable reception, publishers promptly re-released it as the latest number of an ongoing series of novels "complete under one cover."

Although formats varied, the stories were nearly all alike. Generally, they were 30,000 to 50,000 words of stirring action, inflated description, and–since authors were paid to fill a predetermined format–padded prose. They dealt with pirates, detectives, highwaymen, bootblacks, and soldiers. They concerned adventure, history, love, war, romance, life in the city and life on the sea. Popular as they were, however, all of these types of stories were outstripped in popularity by the Western. After classifying stories published by Beadle and Adams alone, Philip Durham concluded that "approximately three-fourths of the dime novels deal with the various forms, problems, and attitudes of life on the frontier, and that more than half are concerned with life in the trans-Mississippi West."[6]

It is difficult, in retrospect, to comprehend the full extent of the popularity that the dime novel enjoyed, but it must have been phenomenal. During banner years, various firms were publishing concurrently as many as 101 different series, and some series ran to more than a thousand titles. Novels with an initial printing of 60,000 to 70,000 copies often went through ten or twelve editions in a single year. For instance, one of the earliest Westerns published by Beadle and Adams, Edward S. Ellis' *Seth Jones; or, The Captives of the Frontier,* sold out of its first printing of 60,000 copies almost immediately; translated into half a dozen languages, it eventually sold more than 600,000 copies.[7] Sales figures similar to these were not uncommon. William Everett, writing in the prestigious *North American Review* in 1864, explained that he had been astonished to learn that by April 1, 1864 "an aggregate of five millions of Beadle's Dime Books had been put in circulation." Such sales, "almost unprecedented in the annals of booksellers," led Everett to conclude that Beadle's yellow-back novels had "undoubtedly obtained greater popularity than any other series of works of fiction published in America."[8] In a similar comment addressed fifteen years later to readers of the *Atlantic Monthly,* W.H. Bishop contended that dime novel and story paper literature presented "an enormous field of mental activity, the greatest literary movement, in bulk, of the age, and [one] worthy of a very serious consideration for itself. Disdained as it may be by the highly cultivated for its character, the phenomenon of its existence cannot be overlooked."[9]

And yet, for the most part, the dime novel phenomenon has been overlooked, especially as it concerns the evolution of the Western. Although Merle Curti made some initial forays into the subject in 1937, it was not until the publication in 1950 of Henry Nash Smith's *Virgin Land: The American West as Symbol and Myth* that scholars began to realize the significance of the dime novel as a cultural document. In recent studies of selected Western heroes, Kent Ladd Steckmesser, Don Russell, and William Settle have attempted to determine the role played by the dime novel in the legend-making process.[10] Still, few attempts have been made to assess the influence of the dime novel upon the development of the Western itself. Unquestionably, the influence was profound. But what was the nature of that influence? Specifically, what influenced the development in the dime novel of those characteristic elements that have since become standard fare in the popular Western?

Certainly, the answer lies somewhere in the interplay of cultural and aesthetic dynamics. In the last four decades of the nineteenth century the United States became an industrialized nation.[11] Between 1860 and 1870 alone, the total number of manufacturing establishments rose by eighty percent, and the value of manufactured products by one hundred percent. In railroads, mining, lumber, meat packing, iron and steel, and oil, whole industries grew up overnight, contributing not only to the national wealth but also to the independent fortunes of a new breed of capitalists—railroad builders like Vanderbilt, Stanford, and Harriman, lumber kings like Weyerhauser, meat packers like Armour and Swift, steel barons like Carnegie and Hewitt, oil men like John D. Rockefeller. Exercising aggressive business practices, and favored by lenient governmental control, these captains of industry engineered the growth of mighty trusts and monopolies that changed forever the nature of American life. Absorbing or eliminating competition, trusts developed in nearly every domain of American industry-in silver, nickel, and zinc, in rubber, leather, and glass, in sugar, salt, and crackers, in cigars, whiskey, and candy, in oil, gas, and electricity. By the turn of the century, the International Harvester Company manufactured nearly all of the nation's farm implements, Standard Oil had a practical monopoly on refining, and United States Steel made two-thirds of the country's steel products. A survey taken in 1904 showed that 319 industrial trusts had swallowed up about 5300 previously independent businesses, and that 127 utilities (including railroads) had absorbed some 2400 smaller enterprises.

For the average American, industrialization and economic growth ushered in a new and uncertain way of life. His food, his clothes, his household furnishings, his tools, the transportation he employed, were made or controlled by trusts. Mechanization threatened to eliminate his job. Affected, too, was the business life of his community. Local shops and industries went out of business, unable to compete with distant corporations. Factories closed, mortgages were assumed by Eastern banks or insurance companies, and more and more of his neighbors gave up their shops and small businesses to go to work for giant corporations whose policies exposed the wage earner to the vicissitudes of vast economic forces. Neighborhoods, too, changed as immigrants arrived in great numbers. Even the nature of the home and family changed as women and children left the home and entered the working world. Between 1870 and 1900 the proportion of women in industry rose from one eighth to one fifth, and the number of child workers between the ages of ten and fifteen rose to one and three-quarter millions. The result of this new and uncertain way of life was that the optimism with which Americans had greeted the first stirrings of the economic revolution in the early part of the century gradually eroded in the years following the Civil War. Optimism continued to be the ostensible mood of the age, but as the deleterious effects of economic growth upon the social, legal, and moral landscape of society became increasingly evident, the average American began to entertain grave doubts about the future.

Around him he saw all of the problems that accompany rapid economic change. Mechanization and the influx of immigrant labor depressed wages while prices spiraled. Severe financial panics disrupted the economy in 1873 and again in 1893. The conflict between capital and labor, long suppressed, at last erupted into the large-scale industrial violence of the great railroad strike of 1877. Strikes occurred thereafter with increasing frequency; from 1881 to 1905 the nation experienced thirty-seven thousand strikes, including the tragic Haymarket riot of 1886, the Pullman strike of 1894, and the Cripple Creek War in the Colorado coal fields. The decline in the quality of life was particularly evident in the crowded cities, where housing conditions were poor, where the crime rate was high, and where prostitution was becoming a serious problem among unemployed working girls. Yet the average American felt that there was little he could do to alter the ominous course of progress. Industrialization, urbanization, class polarization, and control of society by big business and the international agricultural market were gargantuan forces which seemingly led to the abridgment of personal freedoms and the decline of traditional morality. But though totally subject to these forces, powerless to effect any real change in his life, the common man could yet find needed diversion in popular fiction. Here, at least, there existed a world where the grim realities of everyday life did not intrude.

Observers of the time were quick to locate the allure of cheap fiction. Reverend Jonathan B. Harrison, after investigating social conditions among mill-hands in a New England factory town in 1880, was convinced that "the only effect of this kind of reading is that it serves 'to pass away the time,' by supplying a kind of entertainment, a stimulus or opiate for the mind, and that these people resort to it and feel a necessity for it in much the same way that others feel they must have whiskey or opium."[12] Mrs. Jennie C. Croly, a humanitarian noted for her efforts to help New York working girls, shared a more penetrating

No. 2   BEADLE'S FRONTIER SERIES

The YOUNG MOUNTAINEER

insight in testimony before the Senate Committee on Education and Labor in 1883. Working girls read pulp fiction, she explained, because "they want something very different from what they have in their daily lives.... They are crazy for something that is outside of themselves, and which will make them forget the hard facts of their daily lives."[13]

Dime novelists, too, were sensitive to the needs of their audience. Eugene T. Sawyer, author of several Nick Carter detective novels and countless stories in Street & Smith's Log Cabin Library and *New York Weekly,* recognized that the primary appeal of sensational pulp fiction lay in its power to transport readers beyond the confines of their commonplace lives. "To a man whose life is measured by yards of ribbon and pounds of cheese, or bounded by the four dingy walls of a counting house," Sawyer explained, "a dime novel is a revelation and a delight. Most of my readers are mere 'supers' on the stage of life.... Nothing romantic ever happens to them. For all these, hungry for something to take them out of themselves, the dime novel provides a thrill per page."[14]

Though dime novelists aimed their stories at a predominantly working-class audience, the appeal of the genre in fact pervaded the entire culture. Dime novels provided a source of entertainment and diversion for any individual of any social class who sought relief from the anxieties of the age. Again, somewhat defensively perhaps, Sawyer explained: "It is not, however, only the 'submerged tenth' who reads cheap stories. I have been into bookshops and seen bankers and capitalists gravely paying their nickels for the same tales their own elevator boys read.... Such yarns are about as good a remedy for brain fag as you could find. They're easy to read and require little effort of the mind. You can read 'The Pirate of the Caribees' when your nerves forbid ethical discussions."[15] Similarly, an author formerly employed by Beadle and Adams argued in retrospect that "It is a mistake to assume that the 'Beadle' appeal was merely to newsboys and bootblacks or the half-baked intelligences of the community. Take the 'Nick Carter' stories for example, and they were to be found in the hands of men of large business interests and public affairs who did not hesitate to acknowledge that they sought mental relaxation in following the marvelous detective's hairbreadth adventures."[16] Clearly, the intrinsic entertainment value of dime novels–arising from their patterned experience of excitement, suspense, and release–provided a variety of mental relaxation that cut across class distinctions and stimulated broad audience appeal.

Yet a study of the evolution of the Western formula in the dime novel suggests that other, less obvious factors contributed to the popularity of pulp stories, and that these factors influenced the nature of the stories themselves. From its initial appearance in 1860 to its demise late in the second decade of the twentieth century, the dime novel Western responded to the anxieties and aspirations of the age–a function clearly reflected in the standardized setting, stereotyped characters, and conventionalized plots which developed in the stories.

SETTING IN THE EARLY DIME NOVEL

In January 1860, only five months before the House of Beadle and Adams published the first dime novel, an anonymous contributor to *The Christian Examiner* revealed in an essay entitled "The Study of Nature" one of the principal cultural conflicts of the nineteenth century. "The life of man is a perpetual struggle with external Nature," the essayist commences, for "all her influences, if untamed and unresisted, are hostile to his full development and perfect growth, to his physical enjoyments and his higher aspirations, and even to his temporal existence." It is through "subjugation of her forces alone that man can achieve the nobler ends of his creation," and the "extent of his victories over Nature is a measure not only of his civilization, but of his progress in the highest walks of moral and intellectual life." Only by subduing Nature may man "vindicate his claim to be called a being, not a thing...."[1]

Yet only pages later the essayist adopts a different stance. Lapsing into conventional Romantic rhetoric, he speaks fondly of man's "inborn sympathy with Nature." Abandoning his earlier argument that man's relationship with Nature is essentially antagonistic, the essayist now proclaims Nature's influences soothing and educative. He who communes with Nature hears "not music only, but profound instruction, in the notes of the song-bird, and the sighing of the pine; for him the voice of the thunder, of the bursting volcano, of the seething ocean, mingle grand and cheering truths with their words of terror."[2] That a learned contributor to *The Christian Examiner* was capable in one breath of speaking of a harsh and unrelenting Nature and yet in the next breath of evoking primitivistic visions of a benevolent and sublime Nature, complete with the "bursting volcano" of an exotic South Sea paradise, attests to the profound cultural double-think characteristic of the popular attitude toward Nature in the last century.

This ambivalence toward Nature resulted from the widespread currency and convergence in the early years of the century of two antithetical bodies of thought, each of which was decidedly eclectic. One body of thought originated in the ancient notion of an apocalyptical land of happiness and plenty which was presumed to lie in the region of the setting sun. First mentioned by Plato, this idea had accumulated by the nineteenth century a number of related ideas generated by Puritan millennialism, the harshness of New World conditions, physiocratic theories, and American nationalism. Together these notions provided a strong rationale for man's subjugation of Nature. According to this persuasion, unimproved Nature presented a physical and moral obstacle to man's predestined realization of a pastoral utopia seated in the West. Directly opposed to this conviction, however, a second body of thought enjoyed wide currency. Combining notions derived from the European concept of the sublime, deism, natural law theory, the Romantic cult of poetic sensibility, and cultural primitivism, this body of thought constituted a persuasive rationale for the preservation of Nature in its unimproved state. These antithetical attitudes toward Nature gave rise to a serious cultural dilemma during the nineteenth century, a time when Americans were watching with mixed pride and wistfulness the disappearance of the American wilderness.[3]

The frontier settings of dime novel Westerns written prior to the middle 1870s reflect this ambivalent attitude toward Nature. When describing the beauties of the American wilderness, dime novelists customarily invoke the conventional rhetoric of the sublime. Beneath this superficial Romantic mien, however, their attitude toward Nature is unmistakably utilitarian and materialistic. Wilderness is prized for its value as potential civilization. Such is the case in one of the earliest and most popular dime novels ever written, Edward S. Ellis' *Seth Jones; or, The Captives of the Frontier,* a story of Indian fighting set in a "remote spot in western New York" at a time when "the tide of emigration was rolling rapidly and surely to the west." "Ere many years," Ellis reminds his readers, "villages and small cities would take the place of the wild forest." Already "the rich virgin soil had been broken, and was giving signs of the exhaustless wealth it retained in its bosom, waiting only for the hand of man to bring it forth." This attitude toward the wilderness setting serves to establish in the novel an epic context in which the events of the story assume historical significance. Each act of individual heroism becomes an integral part of a grand historical process in which mankind is moving irrepressibly westward, conquering the wilderness and raising in its place a thriving civilization.

The major impetus behind this progressive vision of westward expansion becomes apparent in *The Hunted Life; or, The Outcasts of the Border,* an 1867 Western by Edward Willett. Hailing the Kentucky landscape as the future site of a pastoral society, Willett describes an old hunter and his wife who, pausing at the crest of a mountain range to survey the "rolling and beautifully timbered country" spread out below them, might well be viewing the Promised Land from Pisgah: "In the distance they could discern a broad and level plain, wonderfully fertile, and abounding in buffalo and elk and all manner of game, a paradise for hunters and an eldorado for farmers." Willett's reference to "paradise" and "eldorado" is characteristic of the Edenic diction and imagery that pervaded the early dime novel. Habitually, dime novelists spoke of the wilderness as a potential paradise, no matter what geographical region they were depicting. As wilderness steadily receded before encroaching civilization, dime novelists merely fixed the locus of paradise farther and farther west. Even as late as 1880, little more than a decade prior to Frederick Jackson Turner's formal proclamation of the closing of the frontier, one dime novelist was still describing Texas as an apocalyptical land of "velvet prairies" and "forest-fringed rivers" where "the sun ever shines and the grass is ever green."

The idea of the West as an apocalyptical land of material plenty and human bliss informs a number of early dime novel Westerns whose thrust is explicitly utopian. Novels of this sort synthesize contradictory Romantic and utilitarian attitudes toward Nature, subordinate primitivistic notions to the dominant enthusiasm for progress, and idealize pastoral utopias that combine the advantages of life in a state of Nature and life in society. Rose Kennedy's *Myrtle, the Child of the Prairie,* for example, takes place in the mythical western city of Wakwaka, a utopian community that joins, in the familiar words of Orestes Brownson, "all of the individual freedom of the savage state with all the order and social harmony of the highest degree of civilization."[4] Wakwaka offers its inhabitants a life of ease and freedom amid the bounties of Nature, whose omnipresent beauties have "expanded the hearts of her people" and exerted an ameliorating influence upon the baser human passions. Hugh Fielding, the novel's protagonist, reflects the physically restorative and spiritually redemptive effects of life in Wakwaka. His "physical powers," we are told, "were exercised and invigorated by his out-of-doors life," and his "spiritual nature was fed with the very honey of existence." In fact, "It was not so much to startle the partridge out of the long grass, or to chase the deer to the cover of the wood, that he slung his gun upon his shoulder, although he kept the house well supplied with the choicest game, as it was to be out alone in the midst of boundless and ever-varying beauty, free to dream and to think, while breathing in life of body and liberty of soul."

Inasmuch as it actually depicts the utopian

society of the future, *Myrtle, the Child of the Prairie* differs from the majority of dime novel Westerns penned during the 1860s. To be sure, the pastoral ideal informs most novels of the period, yet dime novelists generally characterize it as a dream which will require substantial effort and sacrifice to realize. Novels in this category are Romantic in their descriptions of wilderness, but they are committed to the values of civilization and progress. Invariably, they invoke the Edenic myth as justification for the destruction of the wilderness and the extermination of the Indian.

Quindaro; or, The Heroine of Fort Laramie offers a case in point. Quindaro, the hero of this 1865 Western, is a confirmed Indian hater who shares the familiar Puritan view of the wilderness West as a second Eden created by God to test and spiritually prepare humanity for the advent of the Millennium. Mary, Quindaro's sweetheart, shares this view. When Quindaro asks her if she wishes to leave her home in the wilderness and enter the civilized world that she has never seen, she replies by describing her dream of a millennial future: "I have read of the 'Garden of Eden,' where our first parents were so happy. And I have pictured to myself even a brighter scene, where *intellect* controls the actions of mankind. But there was a serpent in Eden. Is there any such where Christian men and women dwell?" Gravely replying that "there is 'no rose without its thorn,' " Quindaro admits that "Society is not free from such serpents as cursed the beautiful garden." Yet, at the moment, neither is the wilderness West, he gloomily concludes, reiterating the conventional Puritan analogy between the savages of the forest and the savagery lurking in the dark recesses of the human heart. The manifold beauties of the wilderness, whose "ten thousand charms no tongue or pen can describe," are "marred by the presence of *savages;* and *blood* stains the face of nature! There are many things in all parts of the world, whether in the crowded city or in the deep forest, to mar the loveliness which abounds on every hand. It appears as if the dark demon, which reigns within man's heart, must manifest itself everywhere–everywhere!" Though grimly aware of the pervasiveness of evil, Quindaro sees in the extermination of the Indian and the conquest of the wilderness a providentially ordered plan for the ultimate redemption of mankind. The conquest of the wilderness constitutes, in effect, a rite of purification. By exterminating the disciples of Satan and restoring the Garden of the New World to its pristine state, man may expunge evil from himself and from the world, thus at last ushering in the long awaited millennial future.

Similar spiritual or moral motives for the conquest of the wilderness often appear in the early dime novel Western in the guise of patriotic zeal. Glorifying westward expansion as a national mission ordained by God, dime novelists customarily celebrated the Manifest Destiny of America. Pioneers, declares Percy St. John, author of an 1868 Western entitled *Queen of the Woods; or, The Shawnee Captive,* were patriots whose "energy was indomitable. Never weary, never conquered, they advanced still onward toward the setting sun, laying first the foundations of home and then of empire." Daniel Boone, the preeminent figure in this national mission, St. John extols as the "patriarch of the wilds," the "great pioneer of power and civilization." And in the still untapped resources of the Kentucky wilderness itself, a "paradise" where man may acquire all of "the necessities and luxuries of life," St. John sees a sure portent of America's future greatness. He describes a rolling plain "which, without having many claims to beauty, has other advantages in connection with it. It is richly fertile, though now overgrown with weeds, reeds, rank grass, with here and there a pecan-bush, a coffee-tree, or a dwarf mulberry; but which, ere many years shall have passed, will have a splendid city in its eastern confines and waving cornfields all around." Closing the novel with a rhetorical flourish, St. John pays tribute to the stout-hearted pioneers who established Boonesborough "in the center of the wilderness, which they were daily bringing into subjection."

In setting their novels on the frontier, that constantly moving imaginary line between wilderness and civilization, dime novelists were merely following the trail that Cooper had blazed a generation earlier. In the *Leatherstocking Tales,* Cooper had employed the frontier setting as a metaphorical neutral ground symbolic of America's destiny. Inasmuch as the frontier was always moving westward across the continent and forward into the future, the frontier setting afforded Cooper a means of exploring the social and moral ramifications of the historical process. Ultimately, Cooper arrived at the sobering conclusion that genuine human progress, meaning moral and social progress, was unlikely if not altogether impossible. In consequence, the course of history could not be otherwise than tragic.

But dime novelists either ignored this

possibility or else subordinated it in favor of an overriding conviction that material progress somehow both assured and signified moral and social progress. Unlike Cooper, who probed complexities and faced without equivocation the tragic consequences of America's total commitment to material progress, dime novelists skirted the darker issues. They told their readers what was most comforting to hear—what, in fact, they themselves doubtless believed–namely, that a utopian future of comfort, happiness, and equality was near at hand. Reflecting the optimistic spirit of their age, they affirmed the essential benevolence of the historical process. From the metaphorical conflict between wilderness and civilization implicit in the frontier setting they had inherited from Cooper, they idealized a future paradise in the West which embodied and thus reaffirmed that same optimistic vision which conditioned their use of the metaphor in the first place. Hence it is not in the least surprising to find the pastoral ideal that is envisioned in the early dime novel Western imbued with such mutually reinforcing popular notions as millennialism or Manifest Destiny. But while the pastoral ideal reaffirmed the culture's aspirations, it also helped to resolve one of the nineteenth century's most agonizing conflicts. For insofar as the realization of the pastoral ideal necessitated the settlement of the wilderness, the long-term attainment of the ideal provided a convenient justification for the short-term exploitation and despoliation of Nature.

"Noname's" Latest and Best Stories are Published in This Library.

FRANK READE LIBRARY

Entered as Second Class Matter at the New York, N. Y., Post Office, October 5, 1891.

No. 44. { COMPLETE. }   FRANK TOUSEY, PUBLISHER, 34 & 36 NORTH MOORE STREET, NEW YORK.   { PRICE } Vol. II
New York, July 22, 1893.   ISSUED WEEKLY.   { 5 CENTS. }

Entered according to the Act of Congress, in the year 1893, by FRANK TOUSEY, in the office of the Librarian of Congress, at Washington, D. C.

FRANK READE, JR., And His Queen Clipper of the Clouds.

PART I.   By "NONAME."

The fugitive settler needed no injunction to make haste. His wife and children were in the wagon, and the honest pioneer was seeking to save the loved ones, who were dearer to him than his own life.

THE HERO IN TRANSITION

i. The Backwoodsman

Within the historical context established by the frontier setting, the Western hero of the early dime novel typically functions as an agent of civilization. A fiercely independent man, he is neither suited to nor comfortable amid the laws and proprieties of the settlement. Instead, he lives a perilous but free life on the frontier. Here he contends with the forces of ignorance and savagery. Always triumphant, he slowly but surely pushes back the wilderness, blazing a trail which his more civilized brothers may follow to a golden age in which a free and equal citizenry, physically invigorated and spiritually purified by close and continual contact with Nature, will someday live in perfect harmony.

Two basic types of protagonists appear in the early dime novel, each of whom personifies one extreme of the ambivalent American attitude toward the wilderness. Modeled after men like Davy Crockett or Lew Wetzel, the ugly white man personifies the possible atavistic effects upon the human character of the moral and social vacuum offered by the wilderness—its dangerous freedom, its absence of institutional controls. If the ugly white man is not an ill-mannered braggart like Crockett, then he is, like Wetzel, a violent and uncouth adventurer who lives by the motto that "the only good Indian is a dead Indian." In contrast, the second type of protagonist who appears in the early dime novel derives from the Daniel Boone or Natty Bumppo prototype. Shrewd but spiritually unblemished, he personifies the Romantic, primitivistic notion that Nature is the handiwork of God. Both of these stock protagonists proliferate in the early dime Western, and both function as agents of civilization whose services have been enlisted on behalf of progress: the violent ugly white man exterminates the Indians, while the saint of the forest guides and protects westering settlers.

In creating ugly white men, dime novelists found no dearth of examples in early Western fiction. In fact, the stereotyped traits of the ugly white man were firmly entrenched by the middle 1840s. Characters cast from this mold were sometimes good natured men whose rustic habits and folksy humor abrogated their lack of social polish. More often, however, they were rough and surly Indian killers driven by a single ruling passion–an insatiable hatred for the red man. Introduced in James McHenry's *The Spectre of the Forest* (1823) and reappearing in N.M. Henty's *Tadeskund, the Last King of the Lenape* (1825), the Indian hater soon achieved wide exposure in popular works by Hall, Flint, Paulding, Bird, Simms, Cooper, and others.[1] In these works the Indian hater is usually the lone survivor of a family massacred by savages. Brooding over his personal tragedy—if not actually imbalanced by it—he forsakes the white settlements and disappears into the forest on a life-long mission of vengeance. Characteristically, the Indian hater's physical appearance reflects his inner turmoil: a wild and distracted light glances from his eyes, and emotion convulses his dark countenance. In some instances his head bears the indelible purple scars of the scalping-knife, a grim detail often used to account for the uncontrollable fits of blood lust to which he periodically succumbs.

The principal historical model for the Indian hater of the early dime novel was Lew Wetzel, the renowned Kentucky scout. In a story first serialized in 1866 in the *New York Weekly* and later reprinted in Starr's American Novels as *Lew Wetzel, the Scout; or, The Captives of the Frontier,* Emerson Rodman recounts the details of the ill-fated Bowman expedition against the Indian stronghold at Chillicothe, and describes Wetzel as "a man young in years, yet with an expression of face and appearance of dress that showed he had much experience in backwoods life." Seldom, however, were characterizations of Wetzel as understated as this. In most instances dime novelists portrayed Wetzel in terms of the familiar stereotype. Edward S. Ellis, introducing Wetzel in 1861 in *The Frontier Angel; or, A Romance of Kentucky Rangers' Life,* characterizes the scout as a man who, "to his dying day, carried out the very letter of the vow he had made, never to let any treaty, flag of truce, or any imaginable pretense, screen an Indian from his vengeance. This terrible resolution he had made for the inhuman butchery of his parents when a mere boy by the savages." Ellis also describes Wetzel's physical appearance in familiar terms, explaining that the scout's "face was nearly as dark as an Indian's and marked

BEADLE & ADAMS' 20 CENT NOVELS.

Vol. II.]   Published Monthly.   [No. 22.

OLD DAN RACKBACK,
The Great Extarminator

BY OLL COOMES.

BEADLE AND ADAMS, 98 WILLIAM STREET, N. Y.

with the small-pox. His eyes were of the fiercest blackness imaginable, and there were few who could stand their terrible glance when angry." To enhance his savage aspect, and perhaps to tantalize the scalp-greedy redskins, Wetzel wears his hair "so long, that when allowed to flow unrestrained, it reached down below his knees."

Throughout the 1860s and into the early years of the following decade, the Indian hater continued to be a common protagonist in the dime novel. Wetzel, of course, provided an obvious historical model, but most dime novel Indian haters clearly descended from ugly white men already familiar to readers of early Western fiction. Nevertheless, the stereotype gradually evolved during this period. In general, the trend was toward the development of a protagonist who, despite his being an ugly white man, possessed traits common to the standard hero of the romance.

In *The Hunter's Vow,* a Beadle Western released in 1864, the Indian hater appears as the protagonist of an initiation story. Young Ham Cass, a pale and bookish boy, witnesses his father's death at the hands of an Indian warrior known as Broadfoot. Though the settlers scoff at Ham's apparently impotent oath of vengeance, the boy develops expertise in all of the wilderness skills, tracks down Broadfoot, and eventually slays him. Inasmuch as he is youthful and educated, Ham Cass marks a considerable departure from the wizened, illiterate, and uncouth Indian hater who more commonly appeared in the early dime novel.

A subsequent Beadle Western, *Quindaro; or, The Heroine of Fort Laramie,* also introduces a young man who takes to the trail after discovering that Indians have murdered his family. "I have had life for life, years ago," Quindaro admits, "but I will not bate one jot of my revenge or cease my work until the accursed race has been blotted from existence. Already my name is a terror to them, but it shall become doubly so. I will pursue them to extermination—the monsters!" Despite his passionate nature, Quindaro possesses many of the characteristics of the traditional hero of the romance: he is young and handsome, and he has a sweetheart, though his singlemindedness and strength of purpose preclude his marrying her. He is also rootless. Asked the whereabouts of his home, he proudly replies: "Among the rocks in the mountains, in the valleys, by the river's side-- anywhere, if duty calls me. Quindaro is like the wild bird, free to go where he pleases."

Like Quindaro, the protagonist of an 1870 dime novel Western entitled *White Slayer, the Avenger; or, The Doomed Red-Skins* is a young man obviously "designed by nature for other and nobler pursuits than that of following the Indians' trail." Nevertheless, he has, "for the time at least, abandoned all else for the destruction of the red man." If it were not for the cruel savages, White Slayer muses, "I might have been a happy man to-day, sitting in a pleasant home, with the sweet music of my children sounding in my ears. But now the dear voices are all hushed—still in the grave—and these red-skinned fiends it was who made me the wretched, purposeless being I am! Ah, it has cost them dear already, but they shall pay more yet ere my loved ones are avenged!" It is especially significant, in view of other developments taking place concurrently in the dime novel, that White Slayer meets rejection when he proposes marriage to Mary Dawson, a girl whom he has rescued from the Indians. Mary is frightened by the avenger's volatile nature, and instead marries a peaceable young settler. White Slayer, disheartened, goes "away again, upon the trail of the doomed red-skins."

Mary Dawson's rejection of White Slayer as a suitable marriage prospect is indicative of a fundamental problem that dime novelists encountered when employing the ugly white man as a protagonist. Although they could ennoble the ugly white man in various ways–they could portray him as young and handsome, as being adept in wilderness skills, as being "designed by nature for other and nobler pursuits than that of following the Indians' trail"–he nevertheless remained too choleric, too unrestrained and bloodthirsty to be a viable romantic hero. As a result, dime novelists after 1870 less and less frequently employed the ugly white man as a protagonist. Instead, they relegated him to a secondary role in stories devoted principally to the exploits of an unassailably virtuous backwoodsman.

Stories of this type commonly relied on a device conceived in *Nick of the Woods*. Unabashedly revealing their indebtedness to Bird's Bloody Nathan Slaughter, the Jibbenainosay, dime novelists introduced a series of Indian haters who, during brief but bloody fits of madness, disguised themselves as half-human beasts in order to terrify and murder Indians. In Albert Aiken's "Red Arrow, the Wolf Demon; or, The Queen of the Kanawha," Daniel Boone is the protagonist, but a considerable portion of the novel details the bloodcurdling acts of "a strange and terrible being, that wore the figure of a wolf and the face of a man." Striking fear into the hearts of all who see him, the Wolf Demon indiscriminately murders Shawnee warriors, always leaving his ghastly "red totem"—three knife slashes in the shape of an arrow—on the breasts of his victims. The Wolf Demon, as it turns out, is none other than Boone's companion, Abe Lark, who when dying explains that his crusade of retribution had been provoked by "remembrance of the wife that the red demons tore from me a year ago...."

Although the Jibbenainosay device offered a facile tool for advancing the plot, its chief advantage to dime novelists was that it enabled them to employ the Indian hater's unrestrained violence as a foil against which to define the character of the saintly backwoodsman, who always displays self-control. The author of *Daniel Boone's Best Shot; or, The Perils of the Kentucky Pioneers,* for instance, takes care to inform the reader that Boone does not kill indiscriminately. His "mission was not slaughter entirely, for he never was the aggressor in the fights he had with the Indians, but only chastised them for their inhuman cruelties to white settlers." All indiscriminate slaughter is instead the work of the "Jubernanesy," an "evil spirit" reputed to be half-man and half-bison. Beneath a buffalo-head mask, of course, the blood-chilling "Jubernanesy" is actually Walter Blackwell, a white settler "made insane by cruel wrongs, and in that condition making himself a terror to the savages of the West...." Clearly, the distinction between discriminate and indiscriminate violence helped to justify the Western hero's role as a killer.

Although the ugly white man–particularly in the guise of Indian hater–gained substantial exposure as the protagonist of the early dime novel, his popularity never seriously rivaled that of his less violent counterpart, the saint of the forest. Indeed, by the publisher's own admission, the first dime novel Western hero was modeled after Cooper's Leatherstocking. Other dime novelists generally followed this precedent. As a result, the protagonist of the Western of this period is most often a self-reliant, naturally noble, backwoods hunter or trapper in the tradition of Leatherstocking and Daniel Boone. On rare occasions these backwoodsmen are young, but in the main they are venerable, dialect-speaking veterans of wilderness life.

Daniel Boone invariably displays these stereotyped traits. In Percy St. John's *Queen of the Woods; or, The Shawnee Captive,* published serially in 1868, Boone is a "tall, spare man" possessed of an "experienced and keen sense of woodcraft.... His eye, however, spoke more than anything else the true character of the man. It was clear, bright, and keen. Not a tree, not a bush escaped his notice. Not a sign of the forest was lost upon him." Frederick Whittaker, author of *Boone, the Hunter; or, The Backwoods Belle,* explains that Boone's "provincial accent was the only disadvantage under which he labored," for his physical and spiritual natures were flawless. The renowned woodsman, Whittaker declares, was a "tall, powerfully built man, lean and sinewy, with a grave aquiline face and piercing blue eyes.... Brave and powerful as was his countenance, there was yet in it an expression of complete and guileless simplicity and honesty, mingled with the opposite quality of great shrewdness." This shrewdness, indicative of superior moral perception, manifests itself in Boone's ability to interpret the cryptic signs of the wilderness. In Paul Braddon's *Daniel Boone, the Hero of Kentucky,* Boone's insight is nothing less than astonishing: "hearing a twig snap conveyed to his acute ear volumes of information." And even the passage of time has no discernible effect upon Boone's natural abilities. "Once more pitted against the dusky heathen" in Joseph E. Badger's *The Wood King; or, Daniel Boone's Last Trail,* the dialect-speaking backwoodsman is decidedly old, as evidenced by "the long, snowy locks that fell below his rude skin cap"; even so, "the weight of years seemed to sit lightly upon his frame," and Boone experiences but little difficulty in outrunning the swiftest Osage warriors.

Almost always elderly, irascible, and cursed with a bothersome dialect–traits no doubt derived from the aged Natty Bumppo of *The Pioneers* or *The Prairie*–the backwoodsman possessed a comic potential which dime novelists readily exploited. Drawing upon established traditions, dime novelists endowed the backwoodsman–whether ugly white man or saint of the forest–with idiosyncrasies common to both Southwestern and Down East strains of American humor. One of the earliest Davy Crockett dime novels, *Kill-bar, the Guide; or, The Long Trail,* for example, reflects the considerable influence of the "Crockett Almanacks." In this story Crockett is the typical roughhewn Southwestern frontiersman, boiling over with braggadocio, who resorts to the traditional longbow when recounting his efforts to elude a lovestruck termagant: "I'm Killb'ar, slid from t'other side of the Rocky Mountains on a greased whirlwind, to get rid of Suke Spoon, who are arter me though she knows I are a married man." Later in the story, when Davy and the novel's credulous heroine are treed by an angry bear, the boastful backwoodsman takes advantage of the breathing spell to relate another "stretcher": "Hyar we are in a kind of a scrape, my little gal! I war in somethin' sich a one myself, years ago, when I war Injun'-huntin' out in Kentucky. Jist as the tree was chopped down, though, thar came up a high wind, which, with the help of my buffler-skin, sent me a-whizzin' cl'ar over the top o' the woods to t'other side." Though certainly the most memorable, Crockett was but one of countless ring-tailed roarers in the early dime novel. By 1870, the character who brashly proclaimed himself half-horse, half-alligator had become a fixture in tales set on the Southern Border.

In contrast to the Southwestern tradition, which derived its humor from tall tales and swaggering self-assertion, the Down East tradition provided comic relief through the presentation of a lowborn character whose unusual appearance and pattern of speech–a highly affected vocabulary marred by mispronunciation and senseless repetition–repeatedly undercut his pretensions to gentility. The protagonist of Edward Ellis' famous Beadle Western, *Seth Jones; or, The Captives of the Frontier,* is a self-reliant, naturally noble backwoodsman, yet he manifests all of the character traits of the traditional Yankee peddler. Possessing "a long, thin Roman nose, a small, twinkling gray eye, with a lithe masculine frame, and long dangling limbs," the backwoodsman introduces himself to newly-settled Alfred Haverland in a voice that is in a "peculiar, uncertain state," and which in moments of excitement makes "sounds singular and unimaginable": "How de do? How de do? Ain't frightened, I hope; it's nobody but me, Seth Jones, from New Hampshire." Informing Haverland of the proximity of Indians, Seth warns, "If you vally that 'ar wife of your bussum, and your little cherubims, (as I allow you've got,) you better be makin' tracks for safer quarters."

As the Western formula evolved in the dime novel, the exploitation of the hero's dialect for comic purposes diminished. Beginning in the early 1870s, dime novelists more and more frequently assigned the dialect peculiar to Southwestern humor either to ancillary, purely comic characters–often the hero's sidekick–or to uncouth ruffians in the ugly white man tradition. Similarly, dime novelists shifted the burden of Down East humor from the hero to incidental characters whose bumbling actions recall David Gamut's behavior in *The Last of the Mohicans*. Nevertheless, this type of character–whether Josephus Doublebee, the Massachusetts greenhorn gone west to "strike somethin' of a romantic nature," or Professor Reuben Springs, who sells exploding alarm clocks to the Indians– served merely as a tool for introducing the comic element no longer associated with the hero. This marked tendency to shift the burden of comedy away from the hero is significant, for it was a change requisite to the establishment of the backwoodsman as a character whose traits more nearly approximated those of the naturally noble and innately superior hero of the traditional romance.[2]

The concept of the hero as an elderly trapper or hunter had long posed major artistic difficulties for the dime novelist. An intrinsic fictional problem arose from the fact that the backwoodsman was, in the first place, simply too old to provide the love interest which the audience demanded and which therefore informed most plots. Further, the backwoodsman's dialect and comic role confined him to a lower class status, a position which doomed him to the bachelor life in an age of genteel sentimental heroines. Both the dime novelist, generally an Easterner, and the class-conscious eastern audience for whom he wrote would have considered it socially improper for the common and boastful, though admittedly virtuous, backwoodsman to marry even the silliest of the anemic, upper class heroines. Like any other popular novelist striving to sell books, the dime novelist tried to satisfy public demand. If the audience wanted a hero capable of participating in the novel's love plot, then it would be necessary, the writer realized, either to reshape the aged, lower class hero which the Cooper tradition had provided, or to find some device for avoiding the dilemma entirely.

Seeking the easiest solution, dime novelists displayed amazing ingenuity in avoiding the problem. A favorite maneuver involved the use of multiple protagonists, one or more of whom was old enough and resourceful enough to dominate the main plot of capture and pursuit, while the other was young enough and genteel enough to satisfy the exigencies of the romantic subplot.

Irona; or, Life on the Old South-West Border opens as young Ross Wellend and his sweetheart, Irona Seraville, accompany two Leatherstocking figures, Ned Nuggens and John Smith, across the desolate plains of West Texas. Almost immediately, Irona falls into the hands of Indians, and Wellend loses his way on the plains. The two Texan hunters then step into the foreground of the tale, dominating the remaining action and rescuing Irona from the Comanches. Meanwhile, Wellend is wandering aimlessly. As events draw to a close, however, he fortuitously reappears–just in time to claim the heroine.

In a few stories of this type the marriageable hero hails from the West; if so, his dapper attire distinguishes him from his less genteel Western companions. Pete Wilkins, the aged, dialect-speaking hunter of *The Mustang-Hunters; or, The Beautiful Amazon of the Hidden Valley,* wears soiled buckskin. But Frank Weston, a marriageable youth born of a prominent Texas family, sports a "broad-brimmed hat of gray felt" and a "black velveteen coat," tastefully complemented by "high boots of varnished leather"and "white buckskin breeches."

Although a native Westerner sometimes figured in stories of this type, dime novelists more commonly introduced a well-bred hero from the East. This situation occurs in *Gunpowder Jim; or, The Mystery of Demon Hollow.* Forty-five-year-old Gunpowder Jim, dressed in buckskin and accompanied by his loyal hound Misery, fills the role of the dialect-speaking hunter. But the marriageable hero of the novel is Edgar Allison, an eastern gentleman traveling in the West. As usual, the heroine, Lotta Anderson, is captured–

first by Indians and later by border ruffians. Enlisting the aid of Gunpowder Jim and another elderly backwoodsman, Button Hole Jack, Edgar rescues Lotta and subsequently weds her. Following their marriage, Edgar and Lotta "often try to induce their trapper friends to change their mode of life, but all their efforts are in vain." The two stalwart woodsmen, politely reminding the lovers that "the leopard" cannot "change his skin," shoulder their rifles and conveniently disappear into the wilderness.

It is worth noting, in passing, that the plot of *Gunpowder Jim* possesses an allegorical dimension common to virtually all dime novels that introduce a marriageable Easterner. Novels of this sort are simply maturation stories set in the West. A young and overconfident eastern tenderfoot makes his way through the wilderness in the company of an elderly and experienced guide, a veteran of wilderness life. Together they seek to rescue a captive heroine. Early attempts to rescue her prove futile, but the hero's contact with the wilderness and his growing friendship with the elderly veteran cause him to abandon his false values and to formulate better ones, an educative process generally symbolized by the tenderfoot's gradual acquisition of wilderness skills. Thus, when the elderly veteran is incapacitated–as he always is, usually getting captured, wounded, or killed–the hero is capable of rising to the occasion. This he does, rescuing the heroine and making her his bride. While this plot embodies an oedipal fantasy, it also allegorizes an optimistic view of history. The tenderfoot's educative contact with the wilderness, his redemption, and his attainment of the heroine express in literary form the popular belief that civilization's contact with the wilderness would strengthen the national character, redeem society, and assure the eventual realization of the utopian ideal. No doubt it is significant, too, that the tenderfoot's maturation requires the sacrifice, or at least the disappearance, of the elderly veteran, who clearly personifies the wilderness.

Although the introduction of dual protagonists–a venerable Westerner and a young and marriageable Easterner–lends an allegorical dimension to the plot, the technique also leaves the story awkwardly bifurcated. A somewhat more satisfactory method of introducing a marriageable hero without reshaping the popular image of the backwoodsman appears in *Seth Jones; or, The Captives of the Frontier.* The hero of the tale is Seth Jones, an aged backwoodsman who speaks the traditional comic dialect. When Mary, the lovely daughter of Alfred Haverland, falls into the hands of savages, Seth strives to rescue her, which he does after a series of temporary complications. But at the end of the tale, while the venerable backwoodsman basks in the praise of the gratefully reunited family, the plot abruptly twists. Seth startles everyone by revealing himself as none other than Eugene Morton–Mary's long-lost, young and genteel suitor–in disguise. First divesting himself of his buckskin garb, then abandoning his Down East dialect in favor of lofty sentimental rhetoric, the transformed hero leads his ecstatic sweetheart to the altar. This plot maneuver, perhaps suggested by Oliver Effingham's masquerade as Edwards the hunter in *The Pioneers,* became a frequently practiced dime novel technique. No doubt dime novelists employed it because it permitted them to concentrate the focus of their tales on a single protagonist who was capable of participating in both the adventure plot and the love plot, simply by changing his clothes.

Although dime novelists could incorporate a love interest in the Western either through multiple protagonists or through disguise and abrupt character reversal, these awkward maneuvers were clearly inferior to the fusion within a single character of the best of both worlds: the wilderness skills and unlimited freedom of the Western hero, and the youth, gentility, and romantic potential of the eastern hero. The trend toward the development of this hybrid hero–a development which demanded, of course, that some traits long associated with the Western hero be abandoned–was gradual. Indeed, it was not until the creation of fictional characters modeled after Kit Carson or Buffalo Bill that a hero of these unique proportions consistently appeared. Still, the beginning of the trend is discernible.

A hybrid hero appeared as early as 1861 in Edward Ellis' *Nathan Todd; or, The Fate of the Sioux' Captive.* Not only is Nathan a Leatherstocking figure who speaks dialect and who shows a strong element of Down East humor, but he displays additionally many of the traits of the genteel Easterner: he is young, speaks elevated rhetoric in the presence of ladies, discourses on religion, and eventually makes the heroine his bride. Yet Nathan was an anomaly in the early dime novel. Although young backwoodsmen occasionally dominated the action of tales penned in the 1860s, their dialect

BEADLE'S HALF DIME Library

$2.50 a year.   Entered at the Post Office at New York, N. Y., as Second Class Matter.   Copyrighted in 1879 by BEADLE AND ADAMS.   August 19, 1879.

Vol. V.   **Single Number.**   PUBLISHED WEEKLY BY BEADLE AND ADAMS,   No. 98 WILLIAM STREET, NEW YORK.   **Price, 5 Cents.**   No. 108.

DARING DAVY, The Young Bear Killer; or, the Trail of the Border Wolf.

BY HARRY ST. GEORGE,

AUTHOR OF "ROARING RALPH ROCKWOOD," "RATTLING RUBE," "OLD HICKORY," ETC., ETC.

Stand back! or so surely as there is a sky above us, I will send your soul unbidden, before the judgment bar. Stand back!"

and comic behavior generally relegated them to inferior social status.

During the following decade, however, the status of the Western hero improved dramatically, a phenomenon evident in the apotheosis of Davy Crockett. Published in 1869, *Kill-bar, the Guide; or, The Long Trail* depicts Crockett as a barrel-chested frontier braggart. When he is not wrestling bears or embroidering the truth, he is eluding Suke Spoon, a lovestruck, rolling-pin-swinging virago. Two years later, appearing in *The Texan Trailer; or, Davy Crockett's Last Bear-Hunt,* the eccentric backwoodsman again reveals his ill-breeding. On one occasion, after disposing of a grizzly bear that has hugged him nearly to death, Crockett turns to the genteel heroine and brashly exclaims, "I've only had a good squeezing.... Howsumever, I've been hugged before, and I've no doubt such a good-looking gal as you have been hugged, too. If I hadn't a blue-eyed little wife, down in Tennessee, I'd be tempted to play the bear to you." With his 1873 appearance in *The Bear-Hunter; or, Davy Crockett as a Spy,* Davy acquires a measure of social polish; he treats women with the utmost deference, and he occasionally prays. Yet this is merely a portent of his vastly improved behavior in 1879 as the young and genteel hero of *Daring Davy, the Young Bear Killer; or, The Trail of the Border Wolf.* Here Davy possesses traits common to the Western hero–he is a master of woodcraft, and he tracks down villains–but he also displays the attributes of the polished Easterner. He is "gallant" and, aside from an occasional "I reckon," he speaks perfect English. Moreover, he commands the attentions of not one but two sentimental heroines, one of whom breathlessly refers to him as "my idol, my king." At the end of the tale, in an act which symbolically corroborates his triumph over the limitations of his humble origin, Davy weds the genteel Rosebud Thornton, and together they commence a new life "strewed with roses."

While Davy Crockett was improving his status throughout the early 1870s, other backwoodsmen of lower class origin were making similar progress, especially in novels penned by Joseph E. Badger, Jr. In an 1871 Western entitled *The Forest Princess; or, The Kickapoo Captives,* two Leatherstocking figures exist side by side. Pete Shafer, the elder trapper, speaks in dialect and furnishes the comic element. Young Uriah Barham, who does not speak in dialect, wins the hand of the lovely Myra Mordaunt. Three trappers appear in *The Border Renegade; or, The Lily of the Silver Lake.* While two of them speak in dialect, the third uses the conventional rhetoric of the sentimental novel, and it is he who weds the heroine. By the middle 1870s, heroes of this type were appearing regularly in the dime novel. Retaining all of their former expertise in the manly arts, they proved themselves equally adept in the social graces: their English was impeccable—or as nearly so as dime novelists could make it—and their deportment in the presence of the gentler sex was beyond reproach.

The transformation of the stereotyped Western hero from an old, dialect-speaking, comic backwoodsman into a young and handsome gentleman who was as much at home in the drawing room as he was in the forest constituted a major development in the Western formula. In part the transformation was a natural aesthetic refinement governed by internal dynamics, an organic change dictated by a problem implicit in the basic components of the narrative formula as initially conceived. As long as the stereotyped hero remained an ugly white man or an elderly, unrefined buffoon, he was detached from the narrative's essential love plot. And although dime novelists could partially remedy this difficulty through multiple protagonists or through disguise and abrupt character reversal, these unwieldy devices strained credulity and flawed the dramatic unity of the tale. But the transformation of the stereotyped hero resolved this problem and produced a more tightly unified, streamlined narrative structure. Endowed with obvious romantic appeal, the refined Western hero unified the two fundamental story lines of the Western—love and adventure.

Yet the transformation of the stereotyped Western hero was perhaps influenced by external, cultural dynamics as well. The hero's abandonment of his lower class dialect and comic propensity, and his corresponding assumption of personal attributes and social prerogatives long presumed to be those solely of the upper class, paralleled the growing popular tendency to question the accepted values of the established social order. In a sense, of course, dime novelists were merely "civilizing" the Western hero for the eastern audience. Yet it was a manner of civilizing that implicitly denied the rigid class structure of the East. In an age of increasing class stratification and declining social mobility, the rise of the Western hero affirmed that the opportunity for social advancement still persisted, provided one had the necessary inner resources.

For although he possessed neither inherited wealth nor formal education, the Western hero evinced a natural nobility that all men recognized and admired. Armed solely with this nobility, he transcended the limitations of his humble beginnings. Consequently, the rise of the Western hero satisfied, if only in fantasy, the increasingly strident popular cry for a homogeneous social order in which the status of the individual depended not on artificial class distinctions but rather on the individual's innate worth as a human being.

The emergence of a refined, socially adept Western hero reflects a more profound change in focus and tone that distinguishes dime Westerns penned during the middle 1870s and thereafter. Prior to this time, dime novelists had defined the Western hero in terms of the wilderness. Such traits as simplicity, humility, self-reliance, and moral insight found expression in the hero's plain speech, his functional backwoods attire, his marksmanship, and his keen woodcraft. An agent of civilization, he was equipped to function in a wilderness setting. Yet the refined Western hero who appeared in the middle 1870s was defined in terms decidedly social. His natural nobility found expression in youth and physical attractiveness, polished speech, drawing room *savoir-faire,* and marriageability. A man of the wilderness, he was nevertheless equipped to function in a social setting. This shift in focus accompanied a corresponding shift in tone. The early dime novel Western had affirmed an optimistic view of the course of history; the setting, characters, and plot functioned together to idealize a utopian future which lent ultimate moral justification to the temporary evils of exploitative western expansion and destruction of the wilderness. In contrast, the dime novel Western during the middle 1870s became increasingly primitivistic. Though still affirming a utopian future, the Western of this period commonly employed the utopian ideal as a foil against which to define the shortcomings of existent society.

To some extent, the evolution of the conventional *ubi sunt* illustrates the changing focus and tone of the Western formula during the 1870s. Part of Cooper's legacy to the Western, the poetic speech eulogizing the passing of the wilderness and the inexorable advance of civilization contributes to the elegiac tone of the *Leatherstocking Tales* by counterpointing primitivistic and progressive sentiments: mourning the passing of the wilderness and the decline of the Indian race, the *ubi sunt* is primitivistic; forecasting the advance of civilization and the eventual triumph of the white man, it is progressive. The integrity of the *ubi sunt* as an artistic device in the *Leatherstocking Tales* thus depends on its irony and balance. Yet dime novelists commonly sacrificed this balance in Westerns written during the early and middle 1860s. In novels of this period the death of an Indian frequently triggers a panegyric to the superiority of the white race and to the glorious progress of civilization. The dying words of An-ga-wam, a Huron warrior in an 1866 Western entitled *The Twin Scouts: A Story of the Old French War,* are typical: "White man...you have triumphed at last, and I see in my fate an emblem of the fate of my nation. As I die to-day, a bloody death, such will be the fate of my nation at the hands of the white man."

In dime novels written during the late 1860s and early 1870s, however, the *ubi sunt* is not nearly so peremptory. Though maintaining a broadly optimistic view of the historical process, the *ubi sunt* of this period acknowledges the baser aspects of the pioneer ethos and balks at the costs of progress. Even so thoroughly progressive a novel as Percy St. John's *Queen of the Woods; or, The Shawnee Captive* employs the *ubi sunt* as a means of criticizing the frenetic materialism threatening to undermine the moral authority of the national mission. When Massaquoit, a noble Shawnee brave, laments the destruction of the wilderness and decries the unjust fate of the proud tribes that "melt away, like snow under the sunrays," his hereditary claim to the land elicits contrasting reactions from two frontiersmen. Nathan Hicks, an unprincipled self-seeker who looks upon Nature's beauties "merely in the light of dollars and cents," derides the Indian's claim and dismisses it arbitrarily. But Ned Harris, an upright man who possesses "an eye for the beautiful in nature," sees justice in Massaquoit's claim. Still, he reasons, change is the first law of Nature; the wilderness must and shall be sacrificed to greater ends, and the Indians' only hope for survival lies in conversion to white ways. While both frontiersmen affirm progress, the implication of their differing reactions is clear; there is a wrong way and a right way to advance the cause of civilization; progress must be dignified by high moral purpose. After 1870 the *ubi sunt* frequently voiced this admonition.

Further evidence of the changing character of the Western during this period appears in

Frederick Whittaker's *Boone, the Hunter; or, The Backwoods Belle,* published in 1873. In this novel Daniel Boone, the godfather of civilization, ironically serves as spokesman for the new primitivism. Formerly Boone had functioned in the dime novel as a willing servant of society; his historically documented distaste for the trappings of civilized life had been suppressed, a practice perhaps attributable to his original characterization in John Filson's *The Discovery, Settlement and Present State of Kentucke* (1784). Yet in *Boone, the Hunter* the indomitable pioneer sounds more like his anti-social predecessor Natty Bumppo. Boone is resigned to his role as God's "instrument to people the wilderness and make the waste places full of people," but he nevertheless voices doubts about the nature of the society that follows in his tracks. Standing on a hilltop with his brother Squire, and awed by the sight of a massive herd of buffaloes thundering across a verdant plain untouched by the hand of man, the usually taciturn Boone is moved to speech:

"Squire," he said softly, "when first I stood on this hill and looked out over the plains of this favored land, five strong brave men stood by me, and we rejoiced together that the Lord had shown us such a goodly heritage. Brother, of those five not one is left, and only I am alive to tell the people of the Yadkin what manner of land this is, and how I was preserved. And yet, brother, I am loth to depart from it and bring back settlers. A few years more, and yonder forest will lie low, while of all that great herd of God Almighty's cattle, not one

> will be found this side of the great river. The ax
> and the rifle will turn paradise into a market for
> men to buy and sell, and you and I brother, where
> shall we be?

Recognizing that he is a martyr to progress, Boone
wonders if his self-sacrifice is worthwhile. For
though he is standing on the frontier and gazing
at the wilderness yet ahead of him, his attention
turns instead to the civilization following behind
him. What he sees in that civilization—rampant
materialism, **greed,** **destruction—negates** his
efforts and jeopardizes the realization of the
paradisiacal future whose imagined glory has
been the principal driving force of his life. Boone's
stance in this scene thus prefigures the
metaphorical stance of the later Western hero.
Though still standing on the frontier, the later
Western hero no longer spearheads civilization's
advance into the wilderness; instead he turns back
toward civilization, resolving to take whatever
individual action is necessary to prevent
humanity from wandering off that narrow path of
righteousness which alone leads to paradise.

    Boone, the Hunter also gives some indication
of the issues that come to preoccupy the later
Western hero. Set in colonial Virginia, the story
explores the Jeffersonian distinction between
natural and artificial nobility. From the outset it is
unmistakable that Boone and his younger brother
Squire are *"natural gentlemen."* Daniel's
countenance displays "an expression of complete
and guileless simplicity and honesty," and though
he is disadvantaged by a "provincial accent," he
speaks "a language surprisingly well-chosen for a
man of his plain appearance." Moreover, "the

roughly-clad hunter" carries himself "with the simple dignity of a prince, for it is in the free woods that a man becomes a true gentleman, and proud of the name." In contrast, city-bred Captain Yelverton, an arrogant British officer, is a gentleman only in the most artificial sense of the word. Though born of noble stock, he is an inveterate gambler and heavy drinker who regards the rude backwoodsmen with ill-concealed disdain. As the plot unfolds, Yelverton and young Squire Boone become bitter rivals for the hand of Annie McArdle. Taking advantage of a gambling debt, the lustful dragoon pressures Annie's weak-willed father into sanctioning his betrothal to the maiden. Squire Boone dedicates himself to preventing the repugnant marriage, and it soon becomes apparent that the rivalry can end only in violence.

At this point a related theme emerges, for Whittaker reveals a consuming interest in exploring the Western hero's position with regard to law and the legal system. When Squire expresses his intention of fighting it out with Yelverton on equal terms, the older and wiser Daniel rejects the plan, cooly warning his impulsive brother that he "must remember we're not in the wilderness now. Thar's law and courts, more's the pity, in this colony, and we can't settle our own disputes with comin' into law." The dastardly Yelverton, however, scorns colonial law. "Bah, what's shooting a man here in the backwoods?" he mutters. "They've no laws here." Not content to let the characters reveal themselves, Whittaker intrudes: "And thus it will be seen what a different opinion two different men entertained of the laws of the old North Colony.

The hunter feared them–the town-bred dandy and gambler despised them." Ostensibly, then, Whittaker introduces law as a means through which to define the respective attitudes of natural and artificial gentlemen; whereas the natural gentleman fears the law, the artificial gentleman despises it.

Yet the ensuing action obscures this distinction. Waiting in ambush, Yelverton shoots Squire and wounds him severely. Again the hotheaded youth favors immediate action, and again Daniel counsels restraint. But it is evident, all the while, that the renowned hunter's scruples apply only to the means used to accomplish Yelverton's demise, for Daniel warns his brother that it is of the utmost importance that the villain be "killed in fair fight before all men.... We are in the colonies now, and the law favors no murder. Be easy with this. The man shall die. *I* have said it." Shortly thereafter, Daniel makes good on his promise. Conceding that he "ain't much used to the law...and it's mighty poor justice, from all I've seen of it," and furthermore that "Wood law and rifle justice is what I'm most used to," Daniel confronts Yelverton and fairly and squarely slays him in a duel.

These events, of course, undermine Whittaker's initial distinction between natural and artificial gentlemen on the basis of their respective attitudes toward law. Contrary to Whittaker's claim, Boone does not fear the law; like Yelverton, he resents it. And, indeed, both men place themselves above the law. The real distinction between the two men, of course, lies in their characters. Yelverton is a moral degenerate who resents the law because it interferes with his own selfish interests. Daniel, endowed with an innate moral superiority, resents the law because it inhibits his freedom to act in the interests of a justice higher than that which conventional law can enforce. To Daniel, who intuitively understands natural law, civil law is an unnecessary shackle. Guided by an unerring sense of right and wrong, adhering to a strict personal code whose informing principle is fair play, Daniel is a natural gentleman whose freedom is unjustly limited by a system of laws designed to control self-seekers like Yelverton.

This very point, of course, had been made long before by Cooper. One of the principal lessons that emerges from the *Leatherstocking Tales* is that laws are expressions of human weakness. As long as human nature remains imperfect, laws will be necessary and injustice will persist. Moreover, since it is highly unlikely that human nature will ever change, and since without moral progress there can be little genuine social progress, it follows that the utopian society of the future must forever remain an elusive dream. To the extent, then, that dime novelists such as Whittaker explored the dual themes of natural nobility versus artificial nobility and moral law versus civil law, they were addressing issues implicit in the Western formula from its inception.

Yet their treatment of these issues was fundamentally different from Cooper's. The dime novel Western differed from the *Leatherstocking Tales* in that its ultimate referent was not the real world. Instead, the dime novel operated at the level of fantasy, where conflicts irresolvable in the real world could find swift and clear-cut solutions. Thus, while Natty Bumppo could only shrug his shoulders and declaim against the wickedness and injustice of the world, the dime novel hero could do something about these problems. He could undertake a moral crusade. He could ferret out evil and destroy it. And he could attack social or legal institutions which were subject to distortion or manipulation and which were in this fashion serving the interests of evildoers. In sum, he could singlehandedly spur moral progress and speed society's evolution toward a utopian future. This was to become the Western hero's chief pursuit in the later dime novel.

It was, of course, a pursuit likely to win the approbation of the masses. America in the nineteenth century was a nation undergoing rapid and profound change. Civilization was encroaching upon the last remaining pockets of wilderness; virgin forests were dwindling as the nation's need for timber and farm land increased, and every year hundreds of thousands of buffaloes fell victim to wealthy sportsmen or to hunters employed by railroad crews laying track deeper and deeper into America's hinterland. Factories were springing up all across the country, attracting a massive tide of foreign immigrants to already crowded urban centers. Yet the pace of change continued to accelerate, giving rise to a multitude of social and moral problems that became increasingly difficult to ignore. By the 1870s, open class antagonism, labor strife, and financial panics attested to the very real existence of inequities and injustices that the idealistic rhetoric of progress could no longer explain away. And like Whittaker's Daniel Boone, a growing number of Americans looked into the nation's urban-industrial future and asked themselves,

"Where shall we be?"

During this time of widespread discontent and doubt, the dime novel Western functioned increasingly as a vehicle for social criticism and spiritual reaffirmation. Reflecting this function, there emerged in the dime novel over the next two decades a succession of stereotyped Western heroes who, while never totally displacing the backwoodsman, rapidly surpassed him in frequency of appearance and degree of popularity. These later Western heroes–the plainsman, the outlaw, the cowboy–vigorously enforced moral standards and vehemently expressed both their resentment of artificial class distinctions and their antipathy toward law. Whereas the backwoodsman had turned his back to advancing civilization and departed deeper and deeper into the wilderness, the later Western hero stood his ground. With a clenched fist, he boldly confronted the future.

ii. The Plainsman

The first of the stereotyped Western heroes to achieve eminence in the later dime novel, the plainsman closely resembled in appearance and occupation the backwoodsman who preceded him. Thus it would seem that the transformation of the Western hero from forest scout to prairie scout was a natural development accomplished without great difficulty; merely by seating the backwoodsman on a horse, and by replacing his trusty flintlock with a percussion-cap Winchester and a Colt handgun, dime novelists could update a hero who already commanded a wide and devoted audience. Yet the plainsman's apotheosis was neither this easy nor this direct, for his resemblance to his backwoods forbear in fact worked to his detriment.

The transition from backwoodsman to plainsman relied in part on the use of an historical personage, Kit Carson, whose reputation as a courageous scout and Indian fighter had been established long before the advent of the dime novel. An orphan raised without formal education on the Missouri frontier, an apprenticed leather worker who deserted his craft to seek fame and fortune in the wild West, Carson lacked the impressive physical endowments of the usual Western hero. Nevertheless, his colorful role in Jessie Benton Fremont's adroitly edited reports of her husband's exploring expeditions vaulted Carson, by the 1840s, into national prominence. During the next three decades there grew up around Carson's exploits a substantial body of literature which, including three biographies and several fictional portrayals, provided dime novelists a ready source of usable material.

Carson first appeared as a fictional character in 1849 in Emerson Bennett's bestseller *The Prairie Flower,* but his role was a minor one, and it was not until later that year, with the publication of Charles A. Averill's hardbound novel *Kit Carson, The Prince of Gold Hunters,* that the renowned scout became a fictional character of significant proportions. In Averill's tale Carson is not the genteel hero central to the love plot, but he is nevertheless the focal point of the narrative. Indeed, drawn as a solitary figure mounted on horseback amid the barren wastes of the prairie, his indomitable spirit etched in every line of his sunburnt face, he towers over the other characters.

He is proud, indifferent to danger, and ennobled by his supreme self-reliance, yet he retains many of the traits of his backwoods predecessors: he is dressed like a trapper, and he is not a genteel and therefore marriageable hero but merely a faithful guide.[3]

It was in this transitional state that Carson entered the dime novel. That his character had undergone no significant development in the years between 1849 and the advent of the dime novel is only mildly surprising, for Charles A. Averill, perhaps aspiring to repeat his earlier success in hardbound format, himself penned several tales for Street & Smith's Campfire Library. Without exception, these tales demonstrate Averill's reluctance to abandon a character type already favorably received. This absence of significant innovation was characteristic of Carson's treatment in the dime novel. From the early 1860s through the 1890s Carson appeared in more than seventy original tales and reprints written by a host of dime novelists, including such adept storytellers as Edward Ellis, Albert Aiken, T.C. Harbaugh, Francis W. Doughty, Julius Warren Lewis, Harry St. George Rathborne, and John R. Musick. Yet Carson nevertheless remained a static character. As a transitional link in the evolution of the Western hero, he retained some traits of the backwoodsman while at the same time displaying other traits which prefigured the eventual development of a youthful nomad of the plains.

Dime novelists were of course cognizant of the pressing need for a younger, more charismatic Western hero, a character who would not only keep pace with changing public taste but who would also function more satisfactorily within the narrative formula itself. While their efforts to make such a hero of Kit Carson were neither consistent nor lasting, indications of their awareness of the limitations imposed by Averill's Carson prototype emerge in nearly every tale in which Carson appears. In 1862, for example, Edward Ellis introduced the famous plainsman in "Viola Vennond; or, Life on the Border," a tale released serially in the *Philadelphia Dollar Newspaper* and later reprinted in Beadle's Dime Library as *The Fighting Trapper; or, Kit Carson to the Rescue*. Kit's role in the tale is minor–he arrives as events draw to a close, just in time to rescue a party besieged by Indians–but his characterization is nonetheless notable. Significantly, he is not cast in the backwoodsman's usual role as the heroine's loyal guide and fatherly protector, a role instead consigned to Vic Vannoven, an amiable old trapper obviously descended from Leatherstocking. Rather, Kit is young, athletic, and handsome, though still called a trapper and clothed in the trapper's customary garb.

Other dime novelists made similar attempts to deviate from the standard fictional characterization of Carson. George Blakelee, writing for The Little Chief Library under the pseudonym C. Leon Meredith, provided his readers a youthful hero by fictionalizing Carson's early life; as the titles imply, *Kit Carson, The Border Boy* and *Kit Carson, The Young Hunter* deal with the illustrious scout's boyhood and early manhood. In one novel written by George L. Aiken, *Kit Carson's Bride; or, The White Flower of the Apaches,* the scout is even permitted to marry.

It is likely, however, that this was not so much a legitimate effort to introduce a marriageable hero as it was simply an attempt to account for the historical fact of Carson's marriage to Mountain Flower, a Cheyenne girl.

Though these novels suggest the extent to which dime novelists chafed under the limitations imposed by Averill's Carson prototype, writers were unable consistently to eliminate from the fictional image of Kit Carson those persistent traits which linked him to the backwoodsman of an earlier era. Even as late as the eighties and nineties, when Carson occasionally appeared as a refined and gallant youth sporting a wide-brimmed hat and a Colt handgun, he was just as likely to appear as a backwoodsman whose character showed no appreciable development beyond the stereotype that Averill had established in 1849. In the 1879 hardbound edition of Thomas Harbaugh's *Kiowa Charley, the White Mustanger; or, Rocky Mountain Kit's Last Scalp Hunt,* for instance, Carson is an aged, dialect-speaking trapper. And again, in *The Boy Rifle Rangers; or, Kit Carson's Three Young Scouts,* a tale penned after the turn of the century, Carson is not a plainsman at all. Rather, he is "a true knight of the wild woods," complete with long rifle and coonskin cap.

Many dime novelists, however, were not content to duplicate endlessly an outdated stereotype. Acutely sensitive to the demands of the audience they served, a growing number of dime novelists sought to create a younger, more refined hero, a character whose traits would be more suitable in light of the Western's changing function in the 1870s. Hence the more innovative writers abandoned the historical Kit Carson altogether, creating instead a series of wholly fictitious plainsmen. Although many of these plainsmen took Carson's name in an attempt to capitalize on the great scout's fame, they all possessed the requisite traits of the new breed of hero: youth, social polish, and a penchant for breaking the law.

Undoubtedly, much of Kit Carson's popularity as a dime novel character stemmed from his real life participation in the opening of the West. Most of the exploits attributed to him by pulp writers were purely fictitious, of course, but others–just enough to lend stories in which he appeared an air of authenticity–could be documented.

Perhaps it was in hopes of finding a real life Westerner with credentials as impressive as Carson's that veteran writer Edward Zane Carroll Judson, popularly known as "Ned Buntline," left New York and journeyed west in the fall of 1869. Initially, Buntline intended to make a dime novel hero out of Major Frank North, commander of three companies of Pawnee scouts engaged in fighting the Sioux. But when Buntline arrived at Fort McPherson, Nebraska, and sought out North, the major declined his proposal. According to legend, the major suggested instead that Buntline write about the man asleep "over there under the wagon."[4] That man was William F. Cody, christened "Buffalo Bill" in recognition of his exploits as a buffalo hunter employed by construction crews of the Kansas Pacific Railroad. After talking with Cody and accompanying him on several scouting missions, Buntline returned to New York to build a story around his newly discovered hero. On December 23, 1869, "Buffalo Bill, the King of the Border Men" began as a serial in the *New York Weekly*.

The story was an instant success, and by 1872 Cody's exploits in the dime novel had earned him such fame that a play, *Buffalo Bill, The King of Bordermen,* written by Fred G. Maeder and based on Buntline's story in the *New York Weekly,* opened at the Bowery Theater. Cody, visiting New York at the time, was so impressed by the performance that he agreed to act in a play which Buntline promised to write. On December 12, 1872, Buntline wrote the play in the record time of four hours; *The Scouts of the Plains; or, Red Deviltry As It Is* opened only four days later. Although the show's two stars, Cody and his friend Texas Jack Omohundro, could not memorize their lines and therefore relied on continual prompting by Buntline, who also acted in the play, the show was a popular success. Critics, on the other hand, did not react so favorably to the show's madcap gunplay and Indian killing. As Cody later admitted, "Buntline, as 'Cale Durg,' was killed in the second act, after a long temperance speech; and the *Inter-Ocean* said it was to be regretted that he had not been killed in the first act." The play nevertheless went on tour during the season of 1873-1874, this time with another authentic Western hero added to the cast–the famous Wild Bill Hickok. The association with Wild Bill was short-lived, however, for the "deadliest shot in the West" had the "demoralizing habit," according to Cody, "of firing blank cartridges at the legs of the supers, often burning them severely and at times almost bringing our performance to a ridiculous close."[5] Eventually, Cody and Texas Jack also

GREAT WESTERN LIBRARY No. 74

BUFFALO BILL'S QUEER FIND

By Col. Prentiss Ingraham

concluded their three year association with Buntline, and struck out on their own to organize Buffalo Bill's Wild West, the show destined to win Cody immortality.

The Wild West show played a significant role in establishing Buffalo Bill as the greatest Western hero of all time. Over a period of more than fifty years, untold millions of people in America and abroad thrilled to the show's dazzling displays of bronc-busting, bulldogging, roping, trick riding, and marksmanship. Although the show revealed Cody's penchant for pageantry–the opening parade of the Congress of Rough Riders of the World, the Indian attack on the Deadwood Stagecoach, the reenactment of Custer's last stand–the show's primary appeal lay in its unprecedented authenticity. Most Easterners had never seen the like, and even Westerners found the show impressive. Mark Twain, after attending performances two days in succession, penned a note to Cody in which he praised the show, explaining that it "brought vividly back the breezy, wild life of the Great Plains and Rocky Mountains, and stirred me like a war song. Down to its smallest details, the show was genuine...it is wholly free from sham and insincerity and the effects it produced upon me by its spectacles were identical with those wrought upon me a long time ago by the same spectacles on the frontier."[6]

As Twain's comment suggests, the Wild West show capitalized on the longstanding eastern vision of the West as a realm that constituted a moral and social antithesis to the East. In contrast to the insincerity, artificiality, and socio-economically enforced uniformity of the East, the

West meant naturalness, simplicity, and individuality. Buffalo Bill, himself one of nature's noblemen, became the chief spokesman for the values of the West. His extravaganza was popular because, as Frederic Remington recognized, it represented "a poetical and harmless protest against the Derby hat and the starched linens– those horrible badges of the slavery of our modern social system, when men are physically figures, and mental and moral cogwheels and wastes of uniformity–where the greatest crime is to be an individual, and the unpardonable sin is to be out of fashion."[7]

Buffalo Bill's theatrical career, and particularly his association with the Wild West show, exerted enormous influence upon the dime novel. Following the publicity surrounding his appearance on the New York stage in 1872, Buffalo Bill's name became magic in pulp literature. Not only was there a sudden upsurge in the number of novels featuring Buffalo Bill, but in addition Beadle and Adams began publishing stories supposedly written by Cody himself. The famous scout may indeed have penned a few, but evidence suggests that the actual author was Prentiss Ingraham, an experienced dime novelist.

In terms of wordage, Ingraham was the most prolific writer of Buffalo Bill stories. Although his contribution to the Cody canon is vastly exaggerated–he is usually credited with 211 of 557 original titles, when in fact he authored no more than 121–it was nonetheless substantial, especially considering the span of years during which his stories remained in circulation.[8] Inasmuch as Ingraham served as a press agent for Cody's Wild West show, his prodigious literary effort on behalf of Buffalo Bill is not surprising. In fact, increases in Ingraham's story production may be linked directly to corresponding increases in Wild West show publicity. In 1892, for example, immediately prior to the staging of the Wild West show at the Chicago World's Fair, Ingraham wrote nine new Buffalo Bill novels for Beadle's Dime Library. The large number of novels whose covers bore color illustrations of the show, and whose pages contained notices of future performances, further suggests a mutually profitable association between the Wild West show and the dime novel.[9] In all, about half a dozen novels, including those written by authors other than Ingraham, actually dealt with the Wild West show itself, and two introduced stars of Cody's extravaganza–Buck Taylor and Nate Salsbury–to the public.[10]

The sometimes overt but more frequently indirect exploitation of the dime novel as a publicity vehicle for the Wild West show had a lasting impact on the fictional characterization of the Western hero. Paradoxically, though Cody's show won popular acclaim because it depicted the people and pastimes of the West with a degree of authenticity previously absent from theatrical productions, it nevertheless surrounded these people and pastimes with an aura of pomp and pageantry. Through his association with the show, Buffalo Bill was himself glamorized, especially by publicity conscious dime novelists. Over a period of years this overt theatricality became an integral part of Buffalo Bill's character in the dime novel.

In 1869, when Buntline introduced the legendary plainsman to the public in "Buffalo

Bill, the King of the Border Men," Buffalo Bill resembled the backwoods heroes who preceded him. Depicted on the cover of the *New York Weekly,* Buffalo Bill is bearded, long haired, and garbed in shaggily fringed buckskin. He carries a pistol in his belt, but he leans on the trapper's customary flintlock rifle. And though he does ride a horse in the story, his morality remains that of the backwoodsman: he delivers temperance lectures to his occasionally intemperate companion Wild Bill Hickok, and he shows no surprise when a gambler turns out to be a villain Despite his rugged demeanor and ungrammatical English, Buffalo Bill thinks noble thoughts and consequently wins the lady of his heart, the exquisite Louisa La Valliere, whom he has rescued from a band of drunken soldiers. Presumably, this is Buntline's attempt to account for Cody's actual marriage to Louisa Frederici, for the dime novel hero of 1869 had not yet attained the social status required to marry a genteel heroine. As Buffalo Bill dolefully declares after rescuing Louisa, "If I see her anymore, I shall love her, and love above my station would be madness and folly." Buffalo Bill does, of course, win Louisa in the end, but this is one of a very limited number of stories in which he is permitted a romantic attachment.

But Buffalo Bill's character changed dramatically in Prentiss Ingraham's novels, all written between 1879 and 1904. Most importantly, the tortured speech that Buffalo Bill had spoken in Buntline's novels yielded to a lofty diction that must have represented Ingraham's conception of eloquence. Dialect continued to appear in the stories, but most often it issued from the lips of Buffalo Bill's companions, especially Wild Bill in the early novels. Other dime novelists, following Ingraham's death in 1904, likewise assigned dialect to Buffalo Bill's companions, thereby substantially altering the image of the Western hero. By elevating Buffalo Bill's speech and assigning dialect to his companions, dime novelists continued to shift those traits long associated with dialect–lower class status and comic behavior–away from the Western hero. Hence they succeeded in improving the status of the Western hero without sacrificing the comic element which they considered important to their stories.

This practice, identical to that formerly employed by writers seeking to improve the status of the backwoodsman, gave rise to a series of comic characters who rode in company with Buffalo Bill. Interestingly, though Buffalo Bill's companions included Little Cayuse, a Piute Indian youth, and Dauntless Dell, an Arizona ranch girl, his comic cohorts were most often dialect-speaking backwoodsmen: Catamount Tom, the hide hunter; Alkali Pete Allen, the homely frontiersman; Old Nick Wharton, the owner of an eccentric mare; and, most popular of all, Nick Nomad, the superstitious trapper who, accompanied by his bony nag Nebuchadnezzar, made the first of many appearances in *Buffalo Bill in the Land of Fire; or, Nick Nomad, the Mountain Wanderer.*

Characters of this type seldom occupied roles crucial to the action of the tale. A noteworthy exception, however, was Old Huckleberry, an aged, dialect-speaking trapper featured in an 1893 Ingraham novel entitled *Buffalo Bill's Spy Shadower; or, The Masked Man of Grand Canyon.*

The reason for Old Huckleberry's unusual preeminence becomes apparent at the end of the story when, after adeptly disposing of a gang of road agents, the old man removes his elaborate disguise and reveals himself to be the young and handsome Buffalo Bill.

Instances such as this in which the trapper assumed a central role were exceedingly rare. A vestige of an earlier era, the trapper added another dimension to the story's appeal, yet usually he remained a minor character whose shabby appearance, long-winded bombast, and bumbling behavior provided comic relief. The habitual introduction of humorous trappers attests, no doubt, to the continued popularity of the backwoodsman even beyond the turn of the century. Yet the practice suggests, too, that the popular notion of the backwoodsman was inseparably linked to humor. As long as the plainsman retained an external resemblance to his backwoods forbears–because of his dialect, his weapons, his humble attire, or his awkwardness in social situations–he could not attain his full potential as either a romantic hero or a serious social critic.

Despite their flaws, Prentiss Ingraham's novels present Buffalo Bill as a character suited to these roles. He bears virtually no resemblance, at least externally, either to the traditional backwoodsman or to the stilted plainsman introduced by Buntline. Instead, Ingraham's Buffalo Bill gambles frequently and displays a flair for the theatrical, a trait that manifests itself in flamboyant attire and numerous costume changes. Moreover, the dashing scout's social bearing is flawless. He treats the gentler sex with utmost courtesy, and cooly pauses in the midst of the most desperate circumstances to bury his dead. Even his mode of fighting is highly civilized; hence duels, such as the one fought in *Buffalo Bill's Double; or, The False Guide,* are common, especially in the later novels.

As these stylized activities suggest, Ingraham's stories make use of all of the trappings of the medieval romance. Although critics generally credit Owen Wister with introducing the chivalric element into the serious Western in *The Virginian,* Ingraham titles such as *Buffalo Bill's Bonanza; or, The Knights of the Silver Circle* and *Buffalo Bill and His Merry Men; or, The Robin Hood Rivals* suggest the extent to which dime novelists were making use of the chivalric tradition as early as 1880. The titles were not always so undisguisedly chivalric, of course, but the stories themselves invariably portrayed Buffalo Bill as a veritable knight errant, a "prince of the plains" who galloped around the countryside in the interests of truth and justice.

Yet Buffalo Bill's acquisition of sophistication and social polish coincided with a growing tendency to engage in questionable activities. Ingraham's Buffalo Bill not only gambles–a spicy pastime in the nineteenth century, and one which may actually have contributed to his appeal–but he even dares at times to place his own concept of justice above that of the law. Invariably the plot provides him a just mandate for doing so; either the army has dispatched him on a lone mission to round up deserters and other wanted men, or a group of impotent citizens frightened by the depredations of outlaws has deputized him as a peace officer. In either case, Buffalo Bill finds ample opportunity to enforce justice singlehandedly. And since he is "schooled...in all the craft of the border, and in mountain and plain-lore, Indian trickery and white man's cleverness," his execution of justice is as "invincible as fate."

It remains clear at all times, however, that it is neither hope of reward nor respect for the law itself that motivates the prince of bordermen; rather, he acts because of his unwavering personal commitment to justice. Addressing a group of townspeople on behalf of himself and his comrades in *Buffalo Bill's Queer Find; or, On a Lone Trail*, Buffalo Bill explains that capturing outlaws "is our sworn duty, and whatever we can do, that we will do." Still, he assures the citizens, "we take no trail simply for blood-money. Duty, not hope of reward, brought us here tonight." Yet it is more than a vague sense of duty that spurs Buffalo Bill to action; it is, as well, his confirmed belief that the conventional legal system is incapable of dispensing justice equitably and expeditiously. He does, of course, pay lip service to the law's demand for a "fair trial," but his true sentiments are more accurately expressed by one of his companions, Kid-Glove Kate. "Like half the farces called trial by jury," Kate laconically remarks to a group of townspeople who have unwittingly convicted an innocent man of murder, "your twelve fools have gone wrong, and would hang the wrong person, kill an innocent man...simply because you do not know who else to accuse." Buffalo Bill harbors a similar disdain for the legal system. Still, he is unwilling to dispense with the forms of law altogether. In consequence, he often finds himself in the awkward position of protecting miscreants from a citizenry so enraged that, as he observes in *Buffalo Bill's Featherweight; or, Apache Charley, the Indian Athlete,* "they'll hang a man on suspicion and give him a fair trial afterward–a sure way of getting at the truth, though rather hard on the man if he happens to be innocent."

Since the alternatives to individual action–either the conventional legal system, with its slow and labyrinthine processes, or lynch law, with its rash and dangerously oversimplified reliance on popular whim–appear ineffectual, it comes as no surprise when Buffalo Bill resolves the dilemma by taking the law into his own unerring hands. He does so in an Ingraham novel entitled *Buffalo Bill's Blind Trail; or, Mustang Madge, the Daughter of the Regiment.* After skillfully capturing a road agent, Buffalo Bill learns that the robber has taken to crime in order to regain gambling losses which have placed the mortgage of his mother's home in jeopardy. Instantly recognizing that the youth is no hardened criminal, and sympathizing with his plight, Buffalo Bill chooses to ignore the legal code and to conceal the crime. The prince of scouts then tracks down the crafty gambler responsible for swindling the would-be road agent, and soon regains the young man's money in an honest game of cards. The fact remains, of course, that Buffalo Bill has placed his individual concept of justice above that of the law, substituting his personal moral code for society's in a manner that was by this time becoming characteristic of the Western hero.

In less than a score of years, then, the fictional characterization of the Western hero changed dramatically, primarily as a result of Prentiss Ingraham's efforts on behalf of Buffalo Bill. The hybrid backwoodsman-plainsman, best exemplified by Kit Carson, soon became a figure of the past. And whereas Buffalo Bill had been in Buntline's 1869 story a crude, buckskin-swathed moralist, he was by the middle 1880s a smooth-talking "prince of the plains," a polished theatrical performer whose behavior was on more than one occasion questionable.

Ingraham's interest in promoting Buffalo Bill's Wild West show, as well as his own career as a press agent and dime novelist, certainly accelerated the pace of change, but the transformation of the Western hero was in fact an organic process already evident in the evolution of the backwoodsman. By emphasizing Buffalo Bill's elegant attire and imperturbable courtly bearing, Ingraham merely advanced a trend initiated long before—namely, the externalization of the hero's innate nobility. As a means of delineating character instantly–good men dressed well and behaved decorously, ruffians did not–the externalization of the Western hero's natural nobility was the artist's inevitable response to the internal dynamics of a narrative formula that exalted plot action over character revelation. Moreover, this practice offered the artist an indirect means of defining the Western hero in terms of his relationship to society and its conventional codes.

Yet the externalization of the Western hero's innate nobility exacted a price. With his exaggerated assumption of all of the trappings of refinement, the plainsman sacrificed that simple humility which had once been so prominent a trait of the backwoodsman. He became theatrical, his appearance flashy, his behavior strained. Oddly enough, this grandiloquence in no way eroded his popularity. Paradoxically, that highly stylized behavior which most readers would have considered hifalutin and artificial had it been exhibited by an Easterner was not distasteful when exhibited by a Westerner. To the contrary, readers recognized in the Western hero a man whose natural abilities had won for him the right to exercise the jealously guarded prerogatives of the upper class. Thus readers revered the Western hero as a self-made man. He offered living proof of the existence of a natural nobility that defied rigid class distinctions. And at a time when virtue seemed more often a hindrance than an aid to success, the refined Western hero emerged as a symbol of hope; he reinforced the popular notion that virtue and ability brought tangible reward.

It is probable, too, that still another factor influenced the development of a visibly refined Western hero. By externalizing the hero's innate nobility, dime novelists produced a protagonist whose courtly bearing masked that volatility which remained a trenchant element of his character—that ominous streak of savagery which the Indian hater had overtly displayed and which thereafter became a subtly suppressed trait of the more polished Westerner. In essence, the refined hero's strict adherence to the rules of social decorum in some measure compensated for his defiance of conventional moral and legal codes. Insofar as his concern for propriety increased in conjunction with his self-reliance and lawlessness, his character maintained a delicate balance between acceptable and unacceptable conduct. Consequently, the Western hero remained palatable to a reading public which, subliminally admiring subversive behavior, was reluctant to challenge consciously its established social values. For although the individual reader identified with the Western hero, seeing the hero's unrestrained expression of individualism as his own, he was unwilling to allow such freedom of expression to anyone but himself. The reader resented the social forms and controls that prevented him from fully exercising his own will, but he realized that such restraints were necessary to prevent others–surely less responsible than himself–from fully exercising their wills. Like any individual in any society, the reader resented the personal compromises and concessions which make society possible. At the same time, he desired the comforts and security of a stable social order. By portraying fantasies of unrestrained individualism within a benevolent historical context–the hero's rigorous observance of social proprieties affirmed the values of society, civilization was progressing toward a utopian future–the Western managed to reconcile the reader's desire for unlimited freedom with his desire for the advantages of life in society. Exploring and exploiting the individual's ambivalent attitudes toward the social contract, the Western exerted and continues to exert an appeal not only American but universal.

iii. The Outlaw

In 1877 there appeared in the dime novel a Western hero who threatened to offend public morality. He was the noble outlaw, the Robin

Hood of the American West. Imbued with all of the color and charisma of his pulp competitors, the outlaw differed from them in one crucial respect: he stood outside the law. Although the plainsman demonstrated a penchant for bypassing legal impediments, he nevertheless remained for the most part a law-abiding member of the community. In marked contrast, the outlaw was a social outcast and confirmed rebel whose attitude toward law was openly defiant.

Outlaws commonly appeared as minor characters in dime novels written in the early 1870s, but not until 1877 did the outlaw first assume the role of hero. At this time the House of Beadle and Adams commissioned Edward L. Wheeler, a veteran dime novelist, to write the initial number of the firm's new Half Dime Library. Wheeler, a flamboyant Philadelphian who wore a Stetson hat, saluted strangers as "Pard," and billed himself "Edward L. Wheeler. Sensational Novelist," responded in fine fashion.[11] Released on October 15, 1877, *Deadwood Dick, the Prince of the Road; or, The Black Rider of the Black Hills* introduced a road agent whose instant popularity stunned even the publishers. Clad wholly in black and seated astride a steed "black as coal," Deadwood Dick is intelligent, handsome, and chivalrous.[12] A deadly shot and skilled equestrian, a master in the art of disguise, he cleverly evades pursuit or tracks down villains–tasks facilitated by a guaranteed annual income of five thousand dollars from his own gold mine. Always gallant, Deadwood Dick brings a blush to the cheeks of the beautiful and yearning women who abound in the novels; usually he resists their awkward advances, but he does

The Deadwood Dick Library

Copyright 1878-1884, by Beadle & Adams Entered at Post Office, New York, N. Y., as second class matter. Mar. 15, 1899

No. 10   THE ARTHUR WESTBROOK CO.
Cleveland, Ohio   Vol. I

OMAHA OLL, The Masked Terror; or, Deadwood Dick in Danger.

BY EDWARD L. WHEELER.

DEADWOOD DICK DECOYED.

marry three times and father two children. Each time, however, his wife's unfaithfulness or death shatters his domestic bliss, banishing him once again to a rootless life roaming the hills with his two valiant sidekicks, Calamity Jane and Old Avalanche, the Indian fighter. In all, Deadwood Dick appears in more than thirty novels penned by Wheeler over a span of eight years. When Wheeler died in 1885, other Beadle and Adams staff writers created Deadwood Dick, Jr., a character whose exploits enthralled readers for twenty years more.

While Deadwood Dick's popularity was swelling the coffers of the House of Beadle and Adams, other publishing houses capitalized on the growing appeal of the outlaw hero. The firm of John W. Morrison inaugurated Morrison's Sensational Series, an entire dime library devoted to bandits. Publisher A. E. Ostendorff issued outlaw stories in The Bob Brooks Library. Stories about outlaws began to appear regularly, too, in Frank Tousey's Wide Awake Library and New York Detective Library, and in Street & Smith's Secret Service Series and Log Cabin Library. Soon no respectable firm was without its own dashing road agent. These outlaws were not always fictitious, either. In the neverending search for new material, dime novelists often turned to historical accounts of the lives of actual western badmen, a practice that disturbed a small but influential number of citizens who denounced the trend as a glorification of lawlessness. Beadle and Adams heeded the demands of moralists by prohibiting its authors from writing stories that dealt with actual outlaws, but the policy was more professed than real. Other firms, particularly those of Frank Tousey and Street & Smith, ignored the public furor altogether, releasing novel after novel that sensationalized the careers of such desperadoes as Jesse and Frank James, the Younger brothers, the Daltons, Rube Burrows, Harry Tracy, Tiburcio Vasquez, Butch Cassidy and the Sundance Kid, Hank Starr, and other lesser known bandits. When in 1883 the Postmaster General threatened Frank Tousey with the loss of second-class postal privileges unless he withdrew some of the more lurid outlaw stories from the market, Tousey cut seventy-seven titles from his Wide Awake Library.[13] Still, as Government vigilance waned, Tousey re-issued these same stories under different titles, and the flow of outlaw tales resumed. By the 1890s, one series that printed a high percentage of outlaw stories, Street & Smith's Log Cabin Library, boasted a weekly circulation of 25,000 to 30,000 copies, and it is likely that other series were equally popular. In fact, outlaw stories continued to be so profitable that in 1901 both Tousey and Street & Smith inaugurated separate series devoted to the adventures of the James brothers. During the next two years a total of 277 novels appeared in Tousey's James Boys Weekly and Street & Smith's Jesse James Stories. By 1903, however, public furor and governmental pressure had become irresistible; reluctantly, the two firms finally agreed to discontinue the publication of all stories dealing with outlaws.[14]

Although a number of factors eventually conjoined to bring an end to the outlaw's infamous career in the dime novel, the popularity he enjoyed for a period of three decades was phenomenal. To some extent, this popularity no doubt stemmed from the outlaw's archetypal identity. Rogues and bandits have exerted considerable appeal in all ages and all cultures, and one might argue that the outlaw, more so than any other Western hero, represents a projection of human concerns more universal than uniquely American. Certainly this universality is undeniable, and it would prove an easy task to trace the bloodline of the Western outlaw back to the numerous devil-may-care European highwaymen–such men as Robin Hood, Claude Duval, Sixteen String Jack, or Tom King–who preceded him in the dime novel and who no doubt influenced his development.

But though the Western outlaw was in one sense a reincarnated archetype, he was in another sense the product of a specific cultural context. Like other incarnations of the Western hero, the outlaw responded to the social imperatives and psychological preoccupations of his age; specifically, he reconciled cultural conflicts arising from the increasing polarization of society, the apparent moral decline of the nation, and the unsettling disparity between conventional law and true justice. In the manner in which he responded to the first two of these conflicts the outlaw was little different from the backwoodsman or the plainsman who preceded him. Like them, he was a man whose natural nobility–evident in every thought, look, and gesture–attested to the inequity of a social hierarchy founded upon artificial distinctions of birth and wealth. Moreover, he was a champion of good whose victories assured readers that virtue would ultimately vanquish the insidious forces of evil. In his mode of response to the popular antipathy toward law and the legal system, however, the outlaw differed markedly from his pulp predecessors.

As a lawbreaker, the outlaw posed a singular artistic problem for dime novelists. Previous Western heroes had either acted in the absence of law or merely bypassed legal formalities in their attempts to execute swift and satisfactory justice. But never before had a Western hero openly defied the law. Never before had a Western hero reacted against societal restraint so violently as to waylay stages and rob banks. How then might this new and virulent strain of rebelliousness be justified and reconciled with the hero's traditional virtue? And how might the outlaw hero be differentiated from that mob of ordinary ruffians who also opposed the law?

Dime novelists solved the problem in two ways. First, they masked the bandit hero's questionable behavior with an impenetrable veneer of respectability, always emphasizing his social polish, courtly manners, and chivalrous conduct toward friend and foe alike, particularly women. Second, they provided him a justification for his rebelliousness. Though his heart was as true as steel, they explained, he had been unjustly persecuted and driven outside the law. Thereafter, a good but dangerously embittered man, he lived solely for revenge.

Once instituted, the vindication based upon persecution and justifiable revenge rapidly assumed the nature of a formal device in the outlaw story. Indeed, so pervasive did it become, and so familiar to readers, that dime novelists merely needed to refer to "a thin smile" or "eyes glowing like coals" in order to suggest a desire for revenge. Seemingly, this obviated any further need to supply character motivation. Yet more significant is the manner in which dime novelists tailored the traditional story of persecution and revenge to their own cultural context, consciously transforming this timeworn motif into a narrative convention that enabled them to instill in the outlaw hero that quality most responsible for his appeal--the violent but morally justifiable rejection of all forms of restraint, especially the law.

It was Edward L. Wheeler who, employing the persecution and revenge motif in the saga of Deadwood Dick, set the precedent which other dime novelists would later emulate.[15] When introduced in the first novel of the series, *Deadwood Dick, the Prince of the Road; or, The Black Rider of the Black Hills,* Deadwood Dick is already a road agent. Though he spends considerable time eluding those who would claim the price on his head, he is actually in pursuit of Alexander and Clarence Filmore, two crafty malefactors who, we are given to understand, figure prominently in the outlaw's mysterious past. As the novel nears its conclusion, Deadwood Dick captures the villains and spirits them off to his mountain stronghold. Deadwood Dick's loyal followers prepare to hang the villains, and merely await a signal from their captain before hoisting the two Filmores into eternity. But that signal is long in coming, for the outlaw chieftain takes time out to justify the deed. Flinging aside his black mask and addressing the crowd, Deadwood Dick reveals that his real name is Edward Harris. An orphan, he had been taken in and raised by the kindly Harris family. But in time this home too was denied him, for the scheming Filmores successfully managed the "accidental" deaths of his foster parents. Then, as executor of the Harris estate, the elder Filmore swindled Edward and his sister out of their share of the family wealth. Moreover, he foully mistreated them. "Finding that this kind of life was unbearable," the outlaw explains, "I appealed to our neighbors and even the courts for protection, but my enemy was a man of great influence, and after many vain attempts, I found that I could not obtain a hearing; that nothing remained for me to do but to fight my own way. And I did fight it." Taking his sister with him, Deadwood Dick explains, he escaped from the Filmores, but not until he had first gone to his father's safe and "purloined a sum of money sufficient to defray our expenses." Though the money was rightfully his, its theft branded him a criminal in the eyes of the law. As a result, the outlaw bitterly concludes, "The Hills have been my haunt ever since.... Now, I am inclined to be merciful to only those who have been merciful to me.... Boys, string 'em up!"

Insofar as it appears in this, the first of the Deadwood Dick stories, the persecution and revenge motif relies principally on a personal dispute: the Filmores persecute Deadwood Dick, and he takes revenge upon them. But the story also has an obvious social dimension in that Deadwood Dick's justification for taking the law into his own hands rests on society's refusal to take a stand against the social evil which the Filmores represent. Were it not for the unresponsiveness of the legal system and the inaction of the public, Deadwood Dick would not have been forced to act on his own. And had he not acted on his own he would not have become involved in the chain of events which ultimately deprived him of his rightful place in the community. Through a kind of emotional transference, then, Deadwood Dick comes to resent not only those villainous individuals who actually precipitated his problems but the whole of society as well.

This anti-social sentiment assumes broader scope in subsequent Deadwood Dick novels. Again and again Wheeler places Deadwood Dick in situations that afford the outlaw an opportunity to attack society at large. Two situations are common, each of which places society in the role of oppressor and Deadwood Dick in the role of misunderstood defender of justice. In the first, Deadwood Dick attempts to aid a party in distress but finds himself hampered by an ignorant populace. This, of course, provokes the outlaw's wrath. In the second situation, Deadwood Dick renounces his life on the road and strives to become a law-abiding member of the community; invariably, however, the unforgiving public persecutes him and drives him back into the hills, where he broods over his unjust treatment and swears vengeance.

This latter situation develops in *Deadwood Dick's Device; or, The Sign of the Double Cross*. The plot involves Deadwood Dick's efforts to maintain ownership of a mine which he has inherited upon the death of a friendly miner. The Howells, the miner's avaricious family, resent Deadwood Dick's acquisition of the property and use all of their vast wealth and power to wrest it from him. The conflict is clearly a class struggle, for Wheeler rather intrusively describes the Howells as "a leading family, both financially and socially--for Leadville, mind you, has its

The Deadwood Dick Library

No. 16   THE ARTHUR WESTBROOK CO.
Cleveland, Ohio   Vol. II

CORDUROY CHARLIE, THE BOY BRAVO; Or, Deadwood Dick's Last Act.

BY EDWARD L. WHEELER.

THEN CHARLIE SPRUNG ... DE QUICKLY, AND STRUCK THE BEAR A TERRIBLE BLOW WITH THE
KNIFE IN THE BACK OF THE NECK.

social world as well as its Eastern sister cities, formed out of that class whom fortune has smiled upon. And surrounded by great superfluity of style, pomp and splendor, they set themselves up as the 'superior class,' ye gods!" Although Deadwood Dick has paid his debt to society in a previous novel and is now attempting to lead a law-abiding existence in the community, the Howells use their influence to prejudice the citizens against him. Soon the servile sheriff makes a rash attempt to arrest the former outlaw. Cornered, his vehement protest that he is "lawfully a free man" ignored, Deadwood Dick regretfully guns down the sheriff's men and effects his escape. But in leaving he utters a fearful warning: "To-night I have been forced again into crime, and am an outlaw, by the decree of the people. Let them look out, for I will not stop now, but they shall learn to fear my name as an omen of death."

Characteristically, the justification for Deadwood Dick's oath of vengeance rests on the grounds that he has been unjustly persecuted by a society which, lacking his own "keen sense of perception," too often honors its enemies and maligns its benefactors. "I am an outcast," Deadwood Dick muses, "and as such I have only to remain. Society or the public at large refuse to receive me. They are everlasting enemies.... They curse me, and drive me about, and I have no choice except between this life and death." Reflecting upon Deadwood Dick's martyrdom, Old Avalanche mutters, "He's bin treated liko as ef he war sum dishonorable coyote, an' ef he ain't got cause fer revenge, I don't know myself." Calamity Jane heartily agrees, and together they join Deadwood Dick in a campaign of terror against the citizens of Leadville.

Significantly, Deadwood Dick's banishment from the community affords him an opportunity to vent his righteous indignation in the form of bitter social criticism. Throughout the Deadwood Dick saga, the outlaw's attacks focus upon the same three interrelated issues which he initially raised in his justification for lynching the Filmores. Repeatedly, Deadwood Dick castigates society for its inability to distinguish between good and evil, and for its inaction in the face of injustice. Further, he points out the iniquity of a social system that sanctions the exploitation of the common man by an unscrupulous ruling class. And finally, he ridicules the legal system, contending that it is fundamentally unjust; while it permits those of wealth and influence to perpetrate the most heinous crimes, it severely punishes the common man for the least indiscretion.

These issues recur throughout the Deadwood Dick novels. In *Deadwood Dick on Deck; or, Calamity Jane, the Heroine of Whoop-Up,* the outlaw hero comes to the aid of an honest miner who feels "that very few poor men are so poor but what they can stand firm for their rights." If there were more men in the country like him, we are told, "there would, undoubtedly, be a change for the better, when every man would, in a greater or lesser degree, have an independence, and not be ground down under the heel of the master of money." In *Deadwood Dick of Deadwood; or, The Picked Party,* the outlaw chief cooperates with a detective to topple the business empire of a "purse-proud aristocrat" who lives by the maxim that "wealth is omnipotent." For his efforts, however, Deadwood Dick is sentenced to death by a drunken judge, and it is only due to Calamity Jane's quick thinking that he manages to escape. On another occasion, while defending the rights of a peaceful Crow Indian whose lands have been usurped in *Deadwood Dick's Claim; or, The Fairy Face of Faro Flats,* the noble outlaw threatens to kill Philander Pilgrim, the local attorney and editor of the town newspaper. "A man is liable to arrest, sir, for uttering a threat!" exclaims the attorney. "Good Blackstone," the outlaw chuckles, "but it don't answer here. If you have ever heard of me you will know that I am the man who has found it right, necessary and convenient to defy arrest."

Certainly the most colorful of Wheeler's lawbreakers, Deadwood Dick was but one of many outlaw heroes whom Wheeler portrayed as martyrs to an unjust social system. Time and again Wheeler concocted vindications based on persecution and revenge to explain his hero's death as a social being and his rebirth as a free individual immune to law. Former detective Fred Brayton, hero of *A No. 1, the Dashing Toll-Taker; or, The Schoolmarm o' Sassafras,* takes to the road as a result of a false conviction for murder. Bill Blake, the embittered protagonist of *Apollo Bill, the Trail Tornade; or, Rowdy Kate from Right-Bower,* accidentally shoots an innocent man while tracking down a band of border ruffians responsible for murdering his family. Pursued thereafter by the "untiring minions of the law," Blake assumes a new identity as Apollo Bill, the road agent. And Sam Hathaway, hero of *Solid Sam, the Boy Road-Agent; or, The Branded*

DIAMOND-DICK LIBRARY

Entered According to Act of Congress, in the Year 1897, by Street & Smith, in the Office of the Librarian of Congress, Washington, D. C.
Entered as Second-class Matter in the New York, N. Y., Post Office, March 7, 1896. Issued Weekly. Subscription Price, $2.50 per Year. March 7, 1896.

No. 175.   STREET & SMITH, Publishers.   NEW YORK.   29 Rose St., N. Y.   5 Cents.

Diamond Dick, Jr.'s Call Down;
Or, THE KING OF THE SILVER BOX.
BY W. B. LAWSON.

-DIAMOND DICK JR.-

~W.B. LAWSON~

"YOU SAY YOU ARE DIAMOND DICK, JR., AND I SAY IT IS FALSE. I AM DIAMOND DICK, JR."

Brows, turns to crime after a gang of desperadoes appropriates his gold mine. Though he plans to waylay them individually and collect the gold which is rightfully his, he finds this impossible and instead demands that the citizens of Placer City restore his gold and pay him protection money. When they refuse, the outlaw and his men "justifiably" reduce the town to a "series of heaps of smoking ashes and charred embers, to tell of the vengeance of Solid Sam."

In all of Wheeler's novels the pattern of action is virtually the same. The story of the hero's persecution and ultimate revenge involves three phases. In the first phase, a good man unjustly persecuted by one or more evil individuals discovers that the legal system can neither protect him nor punish his oppressors. Usually the story attributes this injustice to the villain's ability to use wealth and influence either to manipulate the law itself or to corrupt those involved in the slow and complex legal process. On occasion, though, the hero simply refuses to entrust his fate to a jury composed of citizens who lack his own moral insight. In the second phase, the hero undertakes individual action to avenge his wrongs. Through a fatal misstep, however, he breaks the law and becomes a social outcast. In some instances the hero does not actually break the law; rather, he is framed by the villain. In the third and final phase, the outlaw's hatred for the evil individuals who initially persecuted him changes to hatred for society in general. This hatred finds expression in violent action against the community. Implicit at all times, however, is the fundamental assumption that such chastisement is merely part of the hero's paternalistic duty as protector of the people and enforcer of true justice.

Although Wheeler introduced the persecution and revenge motif as a means of characterizing fictional outlaws, other dime novelists soon appropriated the device in an effort to canonize actual Western badmen. Seizing upon those few biographical facts which were germane to the convention, and shamelessly altering those that were not, dime novelists portrayed famous outlaws of the West as victims of an oppressive social system. Nowhere is this process more conspicuous than in the development of the legend surrounding California's most celebrated bandit, Joaquin Murieta.

In all, Joaquin Murieta figured in eight dime novels, seven of which issued from the pen of one man, Joseph E. Badger, Jr., a veteran dime novelist in the employ of Beadle and Adams. Embellishing the rudiments of the Murieta legend as he found them in John Rollin "Yellow Bird" Ridge's *The Life and Adventures of Joaquin Murieta, The Celebrated California Bandit* (1854) and in a pirated version of Ridge's narrative serialized in the *Police Gazette* (1859), Badger gradually added to the Murieta legend those standardized components common to the persecution and revenge motif in the dime novel. In a span of only eleven years, Badger successfully transformed a vicious outlaw into a noble victim of social injustice.

Badger's first Murieta novel, *The Man-Hunters; or, The Scourge of the Mines* (1871), introduces the California bandit as a "famous and desperate highwayman, a demon incarnate." Badger makes no attempt whatsoever to justify Murieta's outlawry; Murieta occupies a minor role in the novel, merely providing worthy opposition to the hero, a roving miner. Yet Badger altered his tactics significantly when he returned to the Murieta legend seven years later. Emulating Wheeler's successful strategy in the Deadwood Dick novels, Badger began to characterize Murieta as a man responding to unjust persecution. In *Three-Fingered Jack, the Road-Agent of the Rockies; or, The Boy Miner of Hard Luck* (1878), Murieta avenges an undeserved whipping. In a subsequent novel, *Big George, the Giant of the Gulch; or, The Five Outlaw Brothers* (1880), Murieta's faithful men defend their leader's lawlessness, arguing that he "was outlawed, a price set upon his head. For what? Because he sought revenge against those who had blackened his whole life.... If he committed crime, if he stained his hands in blood, had he no excuse?" A similar justification occurs in *The Boy Pards; or, Dainty Lance Unmasks* (1881). Though he opposes the titular hero, Murieta is "not all evil." Moreover, he is now "a model of manly grace and beauty," and his voice is as "soft and musical as that of a woman."

At this point Badger apparently determined in earnest to canonize Murieta as a dime novel hero, for his next three novels assumed the classic structure of conventional persecution and revenge. *Joaquin, the Saddle King. A Romance of Murieta's First Fight* (1881) pits the youthful Murieta, a poor but naturally noble vaquero, against the rich and villainous Don Manuel Camplido, Joaquin's rival for the hand of Carmela Felix. In an attempt to discredit Murieta, Camplido hires a band of assassins to murder Carmela's father and to stack the evidence against Joaquin. The conspiracy succeeds, and the outraged townspeople brand Joaquin a "murderous outlaw." Unjustly condemned, deprived of his rightful place in the community, Murieta swears vengeance against Camplido. The bitter struggle between the two rivals continues in a sequel, *Joaquin, The Terrible. The True History of the Three Bitter Blows that Changed an Honest Man to a Merciless Demon* (1881). In this tale Badger dramatizes incidents from the Ridge narrative but explains them in terms of his own melodramatic plot. It is Camplido, we are told, who whips and publicly humiliates Joaquin, who hangs Joaquin's brother on a trumped-up charge of horse-stealing, and who rapes and murders Carmela. Is it any wonder, Badger asks, that Murieta afterward embarked on a bloody career? "I am no apologist for crime... but I firmly believe that not one man out of a hundred, who really possessed the *spirit of a man,* would have turned out any better than he, provided they were forced to pass through the same fiery ordeal, and were as innocent of wrong as was Joaquin Murieta when the blows began to fall." In Badger's last Murieta novel, *The Pirate of the Placers; or, Joaquin's Death-Hunt* (1882), the outlaw's festering hatred for Camplido changes to hatred for society at large. Resorting to the same technique that Wheeler had employed successfully in the Deadwood Dick novels, Badger implements conventional persecution and revenge to create a situation which affords Murieta an opportunity to attack society itself. In the tale that results, Camplido characteristically uses his vast wealth to gain control of the town of Marysville. Disguising himself as a parson, he then prejudices the credulous public against Murieta, convincing the angry citizens to organize a Vigilance Committee to track down the outcast. Since the citizens have "thrown down the gauntlet," Joaquin has no choice but to respond; accordingly, he sets fire to the local gambling hall. Then, as a stiff wind sweeps the flames across the entire town, the audacious outlaw's voice rings out defiantly in the night air: "Men of Marysville, this is the work of Joaquin Murieta! You set out to hunt him from the face of the earth–he shows you that he knows how to strike back!"

Joaquin Murieta's transformation from badman to social rebel parallels the dime novel careers of other historical outlaws. The exploits of Jesse and Frank James, for example, rendered these two outlaws suitable as dime novel heroes. Legend had endowed them with perennial youth, dash, and charisma, and actual incidents in their lives fortuitously corresponded to the conventional motif of persecution and revenge. Legend claimed that Yankee invaders had bound and savagely beaten Jesse during the Civil War. Then, too, since the James brothers had ridden with Quantrill's guerrillas, they were reputedly excluded from the general pardon extended at war's end, and thus forced into outlawry. And finally, in a documented incident, Pinkerton detectives had attacked the James homestead in hopes of capturing the outlaw brothers, but had succeeded only in maiming the boys' mother and killing their younger brother. Yet despite this provocation, legend asserted, the James boys merely robbed the rich to give to the poor.

Recognizing the source of the James boys' appeal, dime novelists unerringly capitalized on

Beadle's Dime New York Library

COPYRIGHTED IN 1881, BY BEADLE & ADAMS.

ENTERED AT THE POST OFFICE AT NEW YORK, N. Y., AT SECOND CLASS MAIL RATES.

Vol. XIII. | Published Every Week. | *Beadle & Adams, Publishers,* 98 WILLIAM STREET, N. Y., December 21, 1881. | Ten Cents a Copy. $5.00 a Year. | No. 165

JOAQUIN, THE TERRIBLE.

The True History of the Three Bitter Blows that Changed an Honest Man to a Merciless Demon.

BY JOSEPH E. BADGER, JR.,

AUTHOR OF "EQUINOX TOM," "SOL SCOTT," "ALABAMA JOE," "JACK RABBIT," "CAPTAIN COOL-BLADE," "PACIFIC PETE," ETC., ETC.

JOAQUIN, THE TERRIBLE.

it. To cite only a single example, in *The James Boys at Cracker Neck* Jesse is generous and extremely courteous to the gentler sex. After waylaying a stagecoach and forcing the passengers to disembark, the blue-eyed and fearless "bandit king of America" refuses to rob a kindly old woman. Instead, he gives her one hundred dollars to aid her sick husband in Kansas City. Later, the "royal bandit" and his men find themselves trapped in an abandoned house surrounded by Sheriff Timberlake's posse. The situation grows desperate, but suddenly Jesse's sweetheart, Zeralda Mimms, arrives with "a party of the best citizens in the Cracker Neck neighborhood and some big officials from a distance who came to rescue Jesse James." Once the citizens have foiled the instruments of institutional law, they remove their disguises and reveal themselves to the celebrated outlaw brothers. Since one of the rescuers is Jesse's "dear old major," and another is an "ex-Confederate colonel," the reader will recall the injustices perpetrated upon the James Boys in the past, and hence excuse their lawlessness.

It is nearly impossible to overestimate the importance of conventional persecution and revenge as a means of justifying the outlaw's rebellion against established social and legal codes. Some such vindication was a vital ingredient in the outlaw's characterization. For although readers were themselves familiar enough with social and legal injustice to understand and identify with a man whom society had forced into rebellion, they could not condone unprovoked lawlessness.

Billy the Kid's failure to attain heroic status in

the dime novel illustrates the public's refusal to condone unjustified violence. Nearly all dime novels that exploited the Kid's career neglected to explain his lawlessness according to the familiar convention. As a result, he remains a consummate villain. In Don Jenardo's *The True Life of Billy the Kid* he is "a fiend incarnate," a "young monster" with a "cold, wicked smile" and "small basilisk eyes" that gleam "like the orbs of a serpent." In J.C. Cowdrick's *Silver-Mask, The Man of Mystery; or, The Cross of the Golden Keys,* the Kid is "a common cut-throat." And in Francis W. Doughty's *Old King Brady and 'Billy the Kid'; or, The Great Detective's Chase,* he is "the bloodthirstiest little cowpuncher what ever straddled a horse."

Only a single dime novel, Edmund Fable's *Billy the Kid, The New Mexico Outlaw; or, The Bold Bandit of the West,* attempted to justify the outlaw's behavior.[16] In this story Billy commences his life of crime only after repeated provocation. Robbed by a "syren" in Silver City, unjustly accused of robbery and thrown into jail, the outlaw declares in a manner reminiscent of Deadwood Dick's earlier protests: "I have tried to do right.... Since I came to this country I have molested no man, and see where I am? Robbed of all my hard earnings, passing my time in this dingy prison, why should I strive any longer for that which in this country seems impossible? I'm done with it." Escaping through the chimney, Billy embarks upon a life of crime. Although this story used the persecution and revenge motif to justify the Kid's lawlessness, the novel was published in Denver by a firm that failed to implement the sophisticated publicity and mass distribution techniques that the major eastern publishers were employing to market less flattering portraits of the Kid. Consequently, Fable's novel went largely unnoticed. And since the eastern firms' more widely circulated accounts of the Kid failed to introduce the persecution and revenge motif to extenuate the Kid's behavior, he never became a recognized hero in the dime novel. Not until years later, when writers fictionalized the Kid's career in hardbound pseudo-biographies, were his anti-social activities rationalized. Only then were readers able to identify with his revolt against social injustice, and only then did they admit him to the pantheon of popular heroes.

Whether used to create fictional outlaws like Deadwood Dick, or implemented as a means of transforming actual western badmen like Joaquin Murieta or the James brothers into misunderstood social rebels, the narrative convention of persecution and revenge enabled dime novelists to provide the American public with heroes who possessed a capacity for resolving in fantasy the otherwise insoluble conflicts of the age. In essence, the outlaw served at least two interrelated cultural needs. On the one hand, he was a projection of the widespread American preoccupation with the meaning and value of law. As a good man victimized by the disparity between that which was morally just and that which was strictly legal, the outlaw hero won a kind of immunity from restraint. Thereafter, guided solely by his own infallible sense of right and wrong, he could resolve the disparity between moral and civil law by taking swift and decisive individual action which insured the execution of true justice. On the other hand, the outlaw hero was a projection of the average American's growing alienation in a modern society characterized by industrialization, materialism, and the suppression of individual freedoms by a rigid socioeconomic structure. Eminently free, the invincible outlaw hero was a man who would not, in Edward L. Wheeler's words, "be ground down under the heel of the master of money." Neither would he stand idly by in an age of apparent moral decline; inevitably, he punished the wicked and triumphed over evil. And if, like an angel of wrath from *Revelation,* he sometimes found it necessary to purify an entire society with thunder and pillars of fire, then this too was just.

iv. The Cowboy

Between 1870 and the turn of the century, while Buffalo Bill and Deadwood Dick reigned as the undisputed co-champions of popular taste, another stereotyped Western hero was rising to prominence. A product of the burgeoning Texas cattle industry, the cowboy first made an appearance in pulp literature in the 1870s. Yet in dime novels of this period the cowboy is merely a minor character introduced to lend authenticity and background color to stories set in the Southwest. During the 1880s and later the cowboy eventually gained exposure as the protagonist of a substantial number of novels, but even in his heyday he never seriously rivaled the popularity of the plainsman or the outlaw, to say nothing of that ageless veteran, the backwoodsman. Yet despite his unimpressive record in the dime novel, the cowboy was eventually to play an important role in the evolution of the Western hero. He was destined to outlast all other dime novel Westerners, and to win international fame as the foremost symbol of the American West.

The cowboy whom history provided dime novelists was in some ways ill-suited to his role in the dime novel. He was neither a professional scout nor an Indian fighter, nor was he an outlaw engaged in robbing stagecoaches and eluding posses. He was merely a ranch hand. For the most part, his life was a matter of hardship, drudgery, and routine. Yet drudgery and routine do not make for exciting reading, and consequently dime novelists did their best to minimize this aspect of the cowboy's life. Though it is not strictly true, as Henry Nash Smith quips, that the dime novel cowboy "apparently has nothing to do with cattle," it is nearly true. Dime novelists make passing reference to round-ups, branding, cattle drives, and other chores associated with the cattle industry, but most of the time they subordinate these activities in favor of exciting confrontations with Indians, rustlers, and other assorted lawbreakers. The daily activities of ranch life merely provide a novel backdrop for the fast-paced plots common to all dime novels.

Deprived of his unique occupation, the cowboy of the dime novel is scarcely distinguishable from the plainsman. Although he is labeled a "cowboy" or "cowpuncher," his distinctive features are largely external: instead of the plainsman's moccasins, the cowboy wears boots and spurs; instead of a hunting knife, he carries a lariat at his belt. Otherwise he is the same. Apparently unwilling to abandon a proven formula, dime novelists characterized the cowboy in the same fashion as they had characterized earlier Western heroes: they continued to externalize the Western hero's natural nobility, and they continued to stress his ambivalent relationship to established social and legal codes.

These practices are evident in the novels of Frederick Whittaker, one of the earliest popularizers of the cowboy.[17] Credit for creating the first dime novel cowboy hero has fallen to Prentiss Ingraham, who fictionalized in 1887 the exploits of Buck Taylor, a star in Buffalo Bill's Wild West show, yet a cowboy hero actually appeared five years earlier in Whittaker's *Parson Jim, King of the Cowboys; or, The Gentle Shepherd's Big 'Clean Out.'* The story concerns Jim Arthur, a consumptive Harvard divinity student who has come west to Muleville, Colorado, to regain his health. In the two years since his arrival the invigorating climate has, to put it mildly, done wonders for him. Within only a year Jim "could run twenty miles in two hours, turn fifty handsprings successively, and had increased his chest girth by three inches." Yet Jim is more than an acrobat. No longer a tenderfoot, the "Gentle Shepherd" has mastered the Westerner's manly arts: he works as an overseer, first of a sheep ranch and then of a cattle ranch; he shoots coins out of the air with his pistols; and, in one of his more impressive displays of skill, he defeats a rowdy cowboy in a duel with bullwhips.

The natural nobility that Jim obviously possesses, and which the outdoor life has externalized, qualifies him for the task of securing true justice for an oppressed citizenry. The town is struggling to escape from the iron grip of The Ranchers' League, a group of wealthy cattle barons who have in the past unscrupulously manipulated the town elections and thus safeguarded their own interests to the detriment of the masses. When election time again approaches, however, Jim Arthur steps forward and announces his candidacy for the legislature, promising just treatment for the "lowly and persecuted cowboy." The cattle barons make a series of attempts on Jim's life, but he foils them at every turn and ultimately wins the election. Vowing to "protect the poorer class of settlers, who have heretofore suffered all sorts of persecutions from the large cattle-owners," the self-proclaimed "champion of the poor" leaves for the State Assembly amid the impassioned cheers of the townspeople.

Similar plots, which offer the cowboy hero ample opportunity to display his natural nobility and to foil wealthy malefactors, inform Whittaker's *Top Notch Tom, the Cowboy Outlaw; or, The Satanstown Election* and its sequel, *The Marshal of Satanstown; or, The League of the Cattle-Lifters*. Set in Texas, these companion stories follow the efforts of the powerful Glasgow Cattle Company to control the local elections and thereby gain legal sanction to fence the open range and deny the country's small ranchers access to water. While Belshazzar Levy, a scheming lawyer, and Berkley, a treacherous English aristocrat, represent the company's interest, the small ranchers find champions in two men whose nobility is natural rather than artificial. Tom Field–reputed to be the deadliest shot in Satanstown, a manly talent which has earned him the sobriquet Top Notch Tom–was raised in the East and trained as a physician. He is also an accomplished singer with "a gift for scribbling poetry and music, which no one but the girls knew of, and which he hid carefully from all the rest of the world." His boon companion, Henry Kimble, the marshal of Satanstown, is a bashful native Westerner known as "Hank the Nailer" in recognition of his ability to drive home nails with bullets. Hank's social polish is less obvious than Tom's, but his latent nobility is nevertheless subtly evinced from the first: the thick Texas drawl that characterizes his speech disappears in the presence of ladies. Events soon confirm Hank's noble nature. He helps to clear Tom of a trumped-up murder charge, routs the company's hired killers, and subsequently aids Tom's successful election effort as the representative of "an indignant people" who, "when forbearance ceased to be a virtue," rose up violently against the mighty cattle corporation. Ousting the cattle barons, Tom and Hank assume control of the cattle company, pledge to keep the range open to all, and marry their respective sweethearts in a dual ceremony.

William G. Patten, another of the cowboy's early popularizers, continued the practice of defining the Western hero in terms of his natural nobility and his opposition to social and legal codes which ostensibly favored the upper class. Writing under his own name, or using the pseudonyms William West Wilder or "Wyoming Will," Patten created courageous men of action: Hustler Harry, the Cowboy Sport; Prairie Paul; Hurricane Hal, the Cowboy Hotspur; Cowboy Steve, the Ranch Mascot; and, Cowboy Chris, the Vengeance Volunteer. Describing his rough and ready cowboy heroes as "good men and true,"

Patten carefully externalized their natural nobility. In *Hurricane Hal, the Cowboy Hotspur; or, Old True Blue's Pilgrimage in Satan's Section,* for example, Hurricane Hal is the hard-driving foreman of the Red Spur Ranch, yet he remains at all times a model of decorum. He and his companion, Maverick Mat, are "faultlessly attired...and, but for the tan of sun and wind upon their hands and faces, they might have passed as gallants of the drawing room, grace, culture, and refinement being shown in every word, look, and motion." Repeatedly, though, Patten's cowboy heroes end up fronting the law. The typical situation occurs in *Cowboy Steve, the Ranch Mascot; or, The Bond of Blood,* where circumstances compel the hero, Silver Spur Steve, to defend a rustler from an angry mob. Training his pistols on the mob while the rustler makes good his escape, Steve rationalizes his actions: "I am not flinging myself in the track of the law," he declares; "I am simply defying lawlessness."

No such glib rationalization can justify the disregard for law displayed by Daredeath Dick, the hero of Leon Lewis' *Daredeath Dick, King of the Cowboys; or, In the Wild West with Buffalo Bill.* Lewis describes his central character as "one of the best marksmen, scouts, hunters, riders, and cowboys, as active as daring, as generous as brave, as gentle and sympathetic in friendship as he was terrible in his wrath," but Daredeath Dick's generosity and gentleness command far less attention than his lawlessness and wrath. After capturing two villainous brothers who have mistreated him, Daredeath Dick declares that he, as a "mob of one," intends to lynch the men. And he does precisely that: "Lighting a fresh cigar,

LOG CABIN

NEW STORIES **LIBRARY** OF STARTLING ADVENTURE

Entered According to Act of Congress, in the Year 1892, by Street & Smith, in the Office of the Librarian of Congress.   Entered as Second-class
Matter at the New York, N. Y., Post Office. March 31, 1890. Issued Weekly. Subscription Price, $5.00 Per Year.   March 31, 1892.

No. 159.   STREET & SMITH, Publishers.   NEW YORK.   31, Rose St., N. Y. P.O. Box 2734.   10 Cents.

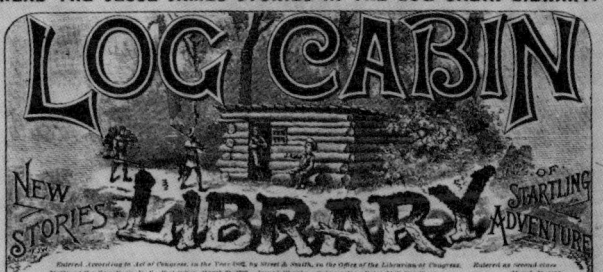

GENTLEMAN JOE THE GILT-EDGED SPORT

" BY JOS. E. BADGER JR.

THE GILT-EDGED SPORT HAD DRIVEN A DAGGER THROUGH HAND AND CASH, PINNING THE GAMBLER FAST TO THE TABLE.

Dick watched the convulsions of the two men until they had ceased, his wild glances gradually becoming less wild, and by the time both forms had become motionless in death, his eyes had become as mild and gentle as those of a gazelle. His desire for vengeance had been appeased! His sense of duty and justice satisfied!" In degree, if not in kind, Daredeath Dick's behavior is atypical. Dime novelists seldom exhibited the cowboy's lawlessness and savagery so overtly. More commonly, they subdued the hero's anti-social behavior and emphasized instead his dashing physical appearance, flashy attire, and exquisite social bearing.

This is particularly true of the most famous dime novel cowboy hero, Buck Taylor, a character modeled after the real life cowboy of that name starring in Buffalo Bill's Wild West. Created by Prentiss Ingraham, Buffalo Bill's press agent and preeminent mythmaker, the fictional Buck Taylor first appeared in 1887 in Ingraham's *Buck Taylor, King of the Cowboys; or, The Raiders and the Rangers*. Though the novel is purportedly an account of the "wild and thrilling" life of Buck Taylor, Ingraham clearly designed it as a publicity vehicle for Cody's show. Consequently, the cowboy hero who emerges in this and subsequent Buck Taylor novels is decidedly theatrical. As we discover in *Buck Taylor, the Saddle King; or, The Lasso Rangers' League,* Buck Taylor sports a dazzling array of jewelry: he wears a miniature lariat coiled around his dove-colored sombrero, a diamond scarf-pin in the shape of a spur, and a horseshoe-shaped ring set with rubies. Supposedly designating Buck's calling, the jewelry is more likely another manifestation of

Ingraham's extravagant taste. Conceding in *The Lasso King's League; or, The Tigers of Texas* that Buck's attire is perhaps a trifle flamboyant, Ingraham admits that Buck "might be called a cowboy dandy." But make no mistake, Buck is "a man to do and dare any deed that mortal could accomplish."

Repeating the tactics he had employed in canonizing Buffalo Bill, Ingraham assigned to Buck Taylor the attributes of the medieval knight. Parallels to the chivalric tradition emerge clearly in the first Buck Taylor story, *Buck Taylor, King of the Cowboys; or, The Raiders and the Rangers,* which recounts Buck's attempt as a young man to enlist in Captain McNally's Texas Rangers. After reporting to the Ranger camp, Buck undergoes a series of trials including boxing, wrestling, and bronc-busting. He demonstrates his skill and courage in each of these events, and is therefore admitted to the elite band of Rangers and permitted to wear their official insignia. The remainder of the story relates the particulars of Buck's quest to save the traditional maiden, in this case Captain McNally's daughter, from the Indians. As Joseph Waldmeir points out in his discussion of the similarities between the Buck Taylor stories and the medieval romance, "initiation into a band of the Chosen by passing tests of physical strength, the gaining of heraldic identification, the quest, courtesy to fallen or disarmed foe (one does not shoot one's enemy in the back), all are part and parcel of chivalric tradition."[18] Subsequent Buck Taylor stories clarify the hero's role as knight errant. At the head of a band of "half cowboys, half mounted scout rangers" employed by the Government as cattle herders and scouts, Buck roams the countryside dispensing frontier justice. He is, Ingraham explains in *The Cowboy Clan; or, The Tigress of Texas,* "the typical Texan cowboy, the *beau ideal* of a reckless, dashing prairieman, a veritable Knight of the Rope."

It is indeed apt that Ingraham nicknames his hero the "Knight of the Rope," for Buck and his entire band carry lariats which sometimes "come in handy for hangman's ropes." Nevertheless, Buck maintains that the majority of cowboys are not lawless, and that the character of the cowboy has been unjustly defamed. These men are reckless and wild, he declares in *The Cowboy Clan; or, The Tigress of Texas,* but they are also "noble in their treatment of a friend or fallen foe." Again defending the cowboy in *Buck Taylor, The Saddle King; or, The Lasso Rangers' League,* Buck talks with a member of the army's Medical Corps, Surgeon Hassam, saying: "I know well that a great many wicked men have crept into the ranks of our cowboy bands; but there are plenty of them who are true as steel and honest as they can be. We lead a wild life, get hard knocks, rough usage and our lives are in constant peril, and the settling of a difficulty is an appeal to revolver or knife; but after all we are not as black as we are painted." Buck's protests prove unconvincing, however, in light of the violent events that unfold in the novels. Buck and his men frequently take the law into their own hands. The typical situation occurs in *The Lasso King's League; or, The Tigers of Texas,* where Buck's band of cowboys, assigned to guard three prisoners, decide instead to hold a mock trial and lynch the men. Later, when a smirking cowboy informs Buck that the prisoners have "escaped," the Saddle King grins at this example of "cowboy justice." Colonel Forsythe, commander of the army post, greets the news philosophically. "Well," he muses, "I can hardly blame them, yet to bring law and order here in this country justice often must be done by illegal methods, and lawless hands work out a certain salvation I suppose."

Apparently most readers agreed, for Buck Taylor soon became the dime novel's foremost cowboy hero. Yet ironically his appearance actually hastened the decline of the cowboy as a distinctive hero type. From the first the cowboy had been divorced from his true vocation as a cattle herder, and thus deprived of that trait which might best have distinguished him from the myriad plainsmen already installed in the pantheon of popular taste. Instead of providing the cowboy distinctive traits, Ingraham merely sensationalized him, endowing him with the chivalric attributes of the plainsman and garbing him in the flamboyant costumes and gaudy jewelry of a dime store mannikin. As a result, the cowboy heroes who appeared in dime novels in the 1890s were little more than plainsmen in chaps, or dandies.

The cowboy-detective Dandy Dan of Deadwood was perhaps the ultimate in fop heroes. Always the epitome of sartorial splendor, this scintillating youth managed to keep his clothes clean in even the most trying circumstances. The opening scene of *Dandy Dan of Deadwood and His Big Bonanza* is typical; although Dandy Dan is tied to a column of stone in the midst of the dusty plains, his clothes are none the worse for wear. He is clad in "a suit of neat black velvet, with patent leather boots on his feet. He wore a white shirt, the front of which was spotless, and in the center of the bosom blazed a magnificent diamond. His broad-brimmed sombrero at his side was gathered up at one corner by a rich cluster of diamonds." Theatrical and flashy, swells like Dandy Dan enjoyed substantial popularity at the turn of the century. As a distinctive hero type, the cowboy's initial challenge to the popularity of other dime novel heroes had failed.

In 1904, however, the publishing house of Street & Smith resurrected the manly cowboy and made the first concerted attempt to establish the cowboy as a hero of equal eminence with the backwoodsman, the plainsman, and the outlaw. In hopes of creating a character capable of competing with Young Wild West, the popular plainsman hero of Frank Tousey's rival Wild West Weekly, Street & Smith launched a new series devoted to the adventures of Ted Strong, an Easterner turned cowboy. Young Rough Riders Weekly, the first continuing series specializing in "authentic" stories of ranch and range life, hit the newsstands on April 23, 1904.

The inaugural issue, *Ted Strong's Rough Riders; or, The Boys of Black Mountain,* penned by Harry St. George Rathborne under the pseudonym Ned Taylor, introduces a cowboy hero calculated to appeal to turn-of-the-century Americans. Modeled after Teddy Roosevelt and obviously designed to capitalize on his popularity as a spokesman for the values of the West, Ted Strong is a gifted athlete and youthful veteran of San Juan Hill who has come to the Black Hills to claim a cattle ranch left to him by his grandfather. Complications ensue, however, when a slick eastern lawyer, Rossiter, and his equally unprincipled son Earl challenge Ted's claim to the Black Mountain Ranch. Rossiter and his men repeatedly provoke violence, and Ted responds by soliciting help from some old friends, a group of eastern boys who, coincidentally, have taken up ranching near Black Mountain. Together, Ted and his friends organize a quasi-military outfit, the "Young Rough Riders," and commence a series of adventures which occupy them for the following 174 issues.

In some respects the stories comprising Young Rough Riders Weekly resemble English boarding school novels or the later Frank and Dick Merriwell stories. Each of the Young Rough Riders is a distinct character, often comic, and schoolboy pranks and humorous episodes occupy considerable space in the novels. Nevertheless, except for tales that appeared near the end of the run when the popularity of the series was dwindling, the stories take place in the West and deal with round-ups, cattle drives, rustling, Indian fighting, rodeos, and other activities associated with ranch life. Moreover, although Ted Strong's long haired companion Bud Morgan is the only native Westerner in the Young Rough Riders, Ted Strong possesses all of the attributes of the Western hero.

Ted's natural nobility is at all times evident. He is handsome, wiry and muscular, "a born leader of men and . . . just about the finest athlete in America." A crack shot and master of trick riding, lariat throwing, and steer roping, Ted manages to come out on top in every contest of skill. On one occasion, in *Ted Strong's Nerve; or, Wild West Sport at Black Mountain,* Ted loses a contest of skill because of skulduggery. Still, he emerges as the clear moral victor.

Like previous Western heroes, Ted Strong is not averse to taking the law into his own hands if he feels that such action is necessary to secure true justice. His occasions for doing so are numerous, for Lawyer Rossiter and his son Earl harbor the Western villain's traditional contempt for the law. Voicing this contempt in *Ted Strong's Rival; or, The Cowboys of Sunset Ranch,* Earl Rossiter cites Rousseau–"a fellow who didn't believe in being bound by any law"–in an attempt to justify his opinion "that a gentleman–a fellow of wealth and culture–need not be bound by the petty laws such as are made for the common herd.... He's able to get away with a good many restrictions, thanks to his money, and he's a fool if he doesn't use it that way."

It is this manipulation of the law by a privileged few that the Western hero stalwartly opposes. Arriving in the Black Hills in the first issue of the series, Ted Strong finds that Lawyer Rossiter, who never forsakes an opportunity to thwart the legal system, has installed one of his own men as sheriff and subjected the honest members of the community to a "reign of terror." But the sheriff and his men make the mistake of underestimating Ted's pluck, and foolishly rustle stock belonging to Ted's friends. In response, Ted proposes the organization of the Young Rough Riders as a band of "volunteer police." Agreeing that this is the only course of action open to them, one of Ted's companions concludes: "There's only one thing to do, boys.... We must take the law into our own hands. We have rifles and ammunition here. We'll organize ourselves into a body of rough riders and we'll patrol this country and defend our own property and try to enforce the law." From this time forth, Ted Strong and his friends set about administering vigilante justice to the cowtowns of the West. In later issues of the series the Young Rough Riders become deputy marshals, thus acquiring a measure of legal sanction for their acts. Still, they show no compunction about stepping outside the law whenever expedience warrants their doing so.

The masthead logo emblazoned on the cover of Young Rough Riders Weekly boasted that the series contained "The Best Wild West Stories Published," but flagging sales eventually prompted Street & Smith staff writers to abandon conventional Western stories in favor of more bizarre plots. As early as 1904, the series' initial year of publication, Ted Strong and his saddlemates were chasing criminals in St. Louis and Chicago. A year later they were rounding up stray camels in the Mojave Desert. Conventional Westerns continued to appear, but at longer and longer intervals. By 1907 Ted Strong was less often on his ranch than on a baseball diamond or polo field, or even aboard a submarine in search of sunken treasure. Clearly, the series could no longer maintain any pretense of being devoted exclusively to Westerns. At last, on August 24, 1907, Street & Smith terminated the adventures of Ted Strong, once again leaving the field open to Tousey's popular plainsman, Young Wild West.

With the demise of Young Rough Riders Weekly the cowboy's brief dime novel career came to a close. In the hardbound books and pulp magazines of a later day the cowboy was to become a popular favorite, but during his heyday in the dime novel he had failed to emerge as a distinct character type. Disassociated from his occupation as a cowpuncher, he had not yet become either a gunfighter or full-time lawman. He was simply a modified plainsman. Like the plainsman, the dime novel cowboy was a naturally noble individual who possessed keen powers of perception that enabled him to penetrate the artificial distinctions of birth and wealth which villains used to cloak their evil designs. Like the plainsman, too, the cowboy felt that law was a cumbersome institution at best, and that the interests of justice sometimes required the abandonment of the forms of law. When this became unavoidable the cowboy acted swiftly, often savagely. Yet his acts were ultimately righteous, and because of him the world was a better place.

The cowboy's demise in the dime novel is indicative of a general slippage in popularity that the Western hero experienced shortly after the turn of the century. Whether cowboy, outlaw, plainsman, or backwoodsman, the Western hero was gradually losing ground to other colorful pulp heroes, principally the detective. As early as 1880, dime novelists adept at penning detective stories as well as Westerns—writers like Edward L. Wheeler and Harry St. George Rathborne—had sent the gumshoe west in pursuit of lawbreakers. There he constituted a worthy opponent for crafty villains, and often, like the Western hero, resorted to operating outside the law in order to compensate for the inadequacies of formal justice. Tracking down villains in the West, and later returning to the sin-ridden cities of the East, the detective soon rivaled the Western hero in popularity. A handful of Westerners like Young Wild West maintained a considerable audience as late as 1928, but new stereotypes of the Western hero failed to emerge. By 1890 the frontier had closed. It would produce no more real-life heroes; its aura of danger and excitement was but a glorious memory. The teeming city was fast becoming the modern wilderness, and the six-gun hero was trapped in an eternalized past.

The character who remained was a man whom Cooper would not have recognized. During the Western hero's long career in the dime novel he had grown from a humble but humorously crude backwoodsman into a polished and defiant social rebel. Gradually, the buckskin-garbed hunter of the pre-dime novel Western tradition had acquired the youth and refinement of the traditional hero of the romance. His virtue and natural nobility had become more obvious, and as he had lost his comic traits and escaped his lower class origin he had assumed a prominent place in the Western's love plot. Moreover, as a plainsman and later as a cowboy he had gained chivalric attributes and a distinct flair for the theatrical. Yet his stylized behavior had served increasingly to compensate for that streak of savagery and rebelliousness which had always been a distinct aspect of his character, and which frequently brought him into conflict with the law.

The changes in the character of the Western hero were, of course, governed by dynamics functioning both within and upon the narrative formula. The intrinsic exigencies of the Western's love plot, for example, in some measure prompted the hero's abandonment of comic traits and his corresponding acquisition of social polish.

Extrinsic economic factors–publicity campaigns promoting Buffalo Bill's theatrical career, or the Government suppression of outlaw stories–likewise influenced the nature of the Western hero.

Yet the most profound changes were expressions of the dominant sociological imperatives and psychological preoccupations of the age. In response to the widespread American longing for a simpler world where men were self-reliant, where individual achievement brought tangible reward, and where social status was the result of intrinsic merit rather than artificial distinctions of birth and wealth, the Western hero gradually developed a visible air of refinement which complemented his natural nobility and thus enabled him to transcend ordinary class limitations. The rustic Davy Crockett who varnished the truth and who offended the heroine's delicate sensibilities disappeared, and in his place emerged a handsome and refined youth who spoke impeccably, who prayed, who could marry whomever he wished. Equally comfortable in the wilderness or the drawing room, he repeatedly proved himself superior as a human being to the self-satisfied plutocrats who oppressed him. In response to the popular fears of moral decline, the Western hero demonstrated acute powers of moral perception that enabled him, like Deadwood Dick or Joaquin Murieta, to ferret out evil and destroy it, even when this meant a desperate and dangerous struggle against public ignorance and apathy. And in response to popular discontent with regard to the inherent inequities of institutional law, the Western hero increasingly displayed a willingness to subvert the law–or to violate it outright–in order to realize true justice.

Like Buffalo Bill, he could distinguish between a hardened criminal and a misguided youth. Like Buck Taylor or Daredeath Dick, he could rescue the oppressed and hang the oppressors.

It is possible, of course, to discern certain relationships between the character traits manifested by the Western hero and the cultural conflicts prevalent in the society that produced him. Yet it is important to recognize that these relationships were not simply direct and causal. Rather, changes in the character of the Western hero resulted from the complex interplay of several aesthetic and socio-psychological dynamics–dynamics which, in the last analysis, remain inextricably interwoven.

Nevertheless, one may discern in the evolution of the Western hero an overall trend toward the development of a stereotyped character whose traits would permit him to carry out more efficiently the principal aesthetic and socio-psychological functions of the narrative formula as a whole. To the extent that the hero's traits came into closer accord with his function in the plot and the conflict implicit in the frontier setting, the Western became a more unified artistic construct. The development of refined heroes like Buffalo Bill or Deadwood Dick, who possessed youth and charisma as well as moral insight and wilderness skills, permitted the hero to assume a central role in the Western's love plot as well as its adventure plot. This fusion of plot lines within a single character (previously,the heroine had been the center of the love plot, the hero the center of the adventure plot) streamlined the narrative structure, rendering obsolete the kind of bifurcated narrative that one so often finds in early Westerns such as *Seth Jones*. Moreover, as the Western hero added eastern social graces to his imposing array of wilderness skills, his character became a more accurate personification of the dialectic between civilization and wilderness implicit in the Western's frontier setting.

The evolution of a refined Western hero also enabled the Western to carry out more efficiently its principal socio-psychological functions. As the prototype hero that Cooper had provided evolved through successive incarnations in the dime novel, he became a more and more accurate embodiment of the ideal world popularly envisioned. The savagery and boorishness which had initially been an adjunct of his wilderness life style yielded to the social polish and cultivated sensibility which civilization alone could produce. Uncouth Westerners like Lew Wetzel disappeared, and a new breed of hero emerged—manly but cultured men like Top Notch Tom or Ted Strong. At the same time, however, the new Western hero rejected the rigid social and legal restraints of civilization and displayed instead the freedom and self-reliance fostered by the wilderness. Like Deadwood Dick, he excoriated existent society, denouncing its injustices and challenging its laws. Like Young Wild West or Buck Taylor, he roamed the countryside and did precisely as he pleased. Hence the Western hero became a hybrid character who synthesized the best of both worlds. He reconciled the popularly cherished values peculiar to the wilderness West with those peculiar to the civilized East, but he espoused none of the unpopular ideas appurtenant to either. Mediating between the antipodal realms of wilderness and civilization, embodying their positive attributes and transcending their limitations, the Western hero blazed a trail to the ideal world envisioned in the dreams and prayers of men.

SETTING IN THE LATER DIME NOVEL

The aesthetic and cultural dynamics that influenced the evolution of the Western hero also fostered the development during the 1870s of a standardized Western setting. In dime novel Westerns written before 1875, plot action normally occurred against a wilderness backdrop. Civilization was sometimes represented in the setting by an isolated settler's cabin, but seldom by more than that. Instead the story followed the fortunes of a small party of pioneers making their way through an alien wilderness environment, either the dense and dangerous forest or the open and equally dangerous prairie. The protagonists of these early tales were agents of civilization, and their antagonists were wild beasts and Indians, personifications of the savage forces of Nature which advancing civilization had to meet and overcome. Invariably, the tone of these early dime novels was optimistic, even utopian, and the dialectic between wilderness and civilization implicit in the frontier setting functioned to idealize a future society that would synthesize the respective values of Nature and civilization.

Beginning in the middle 1870s, however, the dime novel's frontier setting began to function in a somewhat different manner. More and more frequently, novels of this period employed the setting as a foil against which to define and simplistically resolve contemporary social problems which seemingly threatened the future realization of an ideal world. Obvious vehicles for social criticism, novels written after 1875 occasionally took place in an unsettled forest or prairie setting, though for reasons which will soon become clear they far more frequently occurred in and around a small but developing frontier community.

The James Boys in No Man's Land; or, The Bandit King's Last Ride illustrates the function of the setting in novels that employed an alien wilderness backdrop. Released in 1891 under the byline D.W. Stevens, but probably written by John R. Musick, the story takes place in a mythical western region called No Man's Land, "a scope of country west of the Indian Territory, north of Texas, east of New Mexico, and south of Colorado and Kansas." Unaccountably overlooked in surveys, and thus "under no special jurisdiction of any State or Territory, this scope of country became a place of refuge for thieves and escaped convicts of all classes." No Man's Land, it soon becomes apparent, is a virtual Hobbesian state of Nature. It is devoid of law, and its inhabitants lack any awareness whatsoever of the obligations and responsibilities implicit in the social contract. Totally uncontrolled, the residents of No Man's

Land are avaricious and violent, and life in this remote region is therefore brutish and short. Though set in this mythical wilderness, the novel clearly looks beyond No Man's Land to society in the United States. No Man's Land merely serves as a foil against which to explore the unsettling disparity between conventional law and true justice.

Despite the title's reference to the James Boys, the novel deals with the plight of Oliver Davis, an upstanding young man falsely accused of murder and sought by authorities in Lima, Ohio. Oliver would gladly return to the States to clear his name, but he is convinced that he would be unjustly persecuted. Asked to explain why he is a fugitive, he laconically replies: "Suffice it to say that I am guilty in the eyes of the law, but innocent in the sight of heaven. The wealthy and the great have hired the newspapers to slander me. Scores of witnesses are ready to swear my life away.... Half a million dollars are ready to bribe judge and jury to hang me, but I will never be taken alive." This note of criticism sounds throughout the novel, and always the targets of invective are the same: entrenched wealth and a legal system too easily manipulated by unscrupulous plutocrats. As the narrator remarks on one occasion, Oliver Davis "had offended a wealthy and powerful family, and his blood was demanded of them...Money is power, and the poor man has little show against the great and rich. He is trampled beneath their feet, as the elephant and ox trample on the insect."

Although the novel bitterly castigates the failures of society and the established legal system, its ultimate judgment of society is affirmative. Conversing with his sweetheart, Minnie Potter, a simple girl who has always lived in No Man's Land and who has no conception of life in society, Oliver maintains the necessity for law and explains the nature of the social contract. When he observes that law "is necessary for the preservation of society," Minnie ingenuously inquires as to the meaning of "society":

> [Minnie] "What's that?"
> [Oliver] "People living together and enjoying themselves. They make laws, and the laws are to protect the weak from the strong."
> [Minnie] "Protect the weak. Why out here if a fellow hasn't got the nerve to protect himself he goes under."
> [Oliver] "That's wrong."
> [Minnie] "No, it's right."
> [Oliver] "It can't be."
> [Minnie] "Well, it's the way they do things here and a fellow must learn to not let any one get the drop on him."

At this point the narrator conveniently intrudes, explaining that Oliver "had no time to instruct her in the laws of moral rights and ethics." In truth, however, it is the novel's setting rather than Oliver's inept explanations that serves to affirm the value of society and the necessity for law. For the absence of law in No Man's Land fosters a climate of violence and fear. "It would be better for me if I were dead," Oliver remarks. "Life here, chased about by everybody, driven by detectives and Indians is hardly worth having." Even the choleric Frank James agrees. Reflecting upon the greed and treachery of his cohorts, he cynically muses, "No man in No Man's Land can be trusted." Such statements serve to clarify the novel's final statement that life in society, while imperfect, is nevertheless superior to life outside of society. This qualified affirmation of society and the value of law finds further confirmation in the story's ending, though the simplistic resolution of the disparity between law and justice is patently absurd. Marrying Minnie and using the million dollars that she fortuitously inherits from her outlaw father, Oliver returns to Ohio, wins acquittal in the courts, and commences a new life as "a rising young lawyer."

Insofar as it employs a wilderness backdrop as a device for exploring contemporary social problems, *The James Boys in No Man's Land* is uncharacteristic of the majority of novels written after 1875. More numerous by far were novels in which plot action occurred against a societal backdrop, usually a mining camp or frontier town complete with a stagecoach or railroad line, banks, newspapers, and saloons. The protagonists of these later stories live either on the fringe of civilization or, in some cases, within its confines, yet they are closely identified with the values of the receding wilderness. Their antagonists are allied with social institutions; they are bankers, lawyers, politicians, newspaper editors, or wealthy landowners with aristocratic pretensions. The pervasive tone of these later Westerns is, at best, cautiously optimistic. Although still defined within the progressive context established by the frontier setting, these Westerns qualify the merits of civilization, pinpoint the failings of existent society, and frequently espouse primitivistic sentiments. In

DE WITT'S TWENTY FIVE CENT NOVELS

THE MOUNTED RIFLEMAN;

OR,

THE GIRL OF THE ROBBER'S PASS.

ROBERT M. DE WITT, Publisher, 13 Frankfort St., New York.

essence, they function as vehicles for social criticism, though simultaneously they affirm the eventual realization of a better world.

The frontier community setting which began frequently to appear in dime novels during the 1870s and which has since become a standard feature in the popular Western facilitated the later dime novel's function of expressing critical but ultimately affirmative social comment. Typically, these novels take place in and around an isolated, newly established town or mining camp situated on the advancing frontier and surrounded by the open prairie of the Great Plains or the deserts and mountains of the Far West. As an outpost of advancing civilization, the town is tenuously linked to the rest of the world by a trail, a stagecoach line, or in some instances by a railroad, and each day more settlers arrive to swell the population of the already bustling community.[1] Most importantly, though still in the early stages of settlement, the town possesses such features as a newspaper, elections, and an established class structure; hence the town is suitable as a microcosm through which to criticize social institutions and to explore the pressing conflicts of a more advanced, urban culture.

Edward L. Wheeler, always an inspired innovator, was the first dime novelist to recognize the artistic potential of the frontier community setting. Though set in such far ranging geographical locations as Deadwood, South Dakota or Leadville, Colorado, all thirty-three novels in the Deadwood Dick series take place in the vicinity of a newly established town or mining camp. Moreover, each of these communities suffers from one or more social maladies also afflicting eastern society—maladies which Deadwood Dick takes it upon himself to cure. In *Deadwood Dick on Deck; or, Calamity Jane, the Heroine of Whoop-Up,* Deadwood Dick rids the mining town of Whoop-Up of an assortment of speculators, shifty politicians, and "capitalists who would like to step down into the little city of Whoop-Up, and grasp the tyrant's reins in their hands." In *Deadwood Dick of Deadwood; or, The Picked Party,* the noble outlaw foils attempts by a "purse-proud aristocrat" to establish a corrupt business empire in Deadwood. And in *The Phantom Miner; or, Deadwood Dick's Bonanza,* the Prince of the Road confronts the disparity between law and justice in the Idaho boom town of Eureka. Insofar as these fledgling frontier communities function as microcosms of eastern society, they refine the Western as a vehicle for addressing social problems associated with urbanization and industrialization.

Yet despite their vehement social criticism, Westerns of this period simultaneously forecast a utopian future. Always bustling with activity and growth, the cowtowns and mining camps depicted in the later dime novel are located on the advancing frontier, where their presence implicitly affirms the continued progress of civilization. To be sure, these newly settled communities are daily confronting the perils associated with progress, and it is this confrontation that gives rise to the numerous conflicts which provide the Western its action. Yet the dime novel portrays these growing communities during what John Cawelti has termed an "epic moment," a time when the social evils which have already corrupted the urban centers of the East have not yet gained a firm foothold. Hence the future of these embryonic societies remains pliant, and their presence in the Western's setting sustains the possibility that a utopian society may yet evolve in the West. Against this optimistic backdrop, the Western hero emerges as the guardian of the future. His stylized acts of violence are in fact rites of purification; each time he resolves a social problem afflicting one of these incipient utopias–by shooting a villain, say, or by foiling a scheming aristocrat–he is taking a positive step toward the eventual realization of a better world. Thus, while the standardized setting of these later Westerns facilitates the expression of social criticism, it simultaneously affirms an optimistic view of the course of history.

In emphasizing the Western setting's socio-psychological function, however, it would be unwise to overlook the setting's equally important aesthetic function. For the landscape of the Great Plains and Far West possesses unusual dramatic potential, and dime novelists unerringly capitalized on it. The region between Council Grove and Santa Fe, Ned Buntline explains in *Sib Cone, the Mountain Trapper,* presents "as desolate a scene as could well be imagined in that lonely region, the prairies of the Far West. As far as the eye could reach, nothing was to be seen but a dry and barren plain, stretching away to meet the embrace of the distant horizon.... Silence and desolation seemed there to reign together.... It is a land of plenty, and of want; of destitution, and of beauty; of life, and of death." An open and seemingly endless landscape of vast grandeur and striking contrasts, the Western setting visually images the dramatic conflicts implicit in the Western formula: the clash between civilization and wilderness, man and Nature, good and evil, and life and death. Against a backdrop of such magnitude, the Western's characters attain epic proportions.

Aesthetically, the unlimited openness of the western landscape is perhaps the most functional aspect of the Western's setting, for open space offers the reader a bird's eye view of the action continually unfolding~often simultaneously~on various parts of the landscape. It is helpful to think of the dime novel Western's standardized setting as a vast gameboard upon which opposing pieces are carefully moved to or from distinct, pre-arranged areas. The Western setting subdivides into three such areas: located in the middle of the landscape, an isolated town or mining camp; surrounding the town, a vast intermediate area of open prairie; and, farthest removed from the town, an outlying camp, commonly a ranch or hideout.[2]

The precise character or moral value of the setting's polarized locales~the town and the outlying camp~differs according to the nature of the conflict and the location of the villain. In the simplest stories the town represents the forces of civilization, progress, and virtue, while the outlying camp harbors antithetical forces, usually Indians or outlaws. This is not always the case, however, for the opposite situation frequently occurs in stories that are, relatively speaking, more sophisticated. Here a villain masquerading as a law-abiding member of the community~ generally a banker or a lawyer~subtly undermines the values of civilization from within, duping the populace and making the town the abode of evil. If so, the outlying camp becomes the locus of positive forces--in most cases noble rogues who, despite their status as outlaws, nevertheless advance the cause of justice and virtue. This situation prevails throughout the Deadwood Dick novels, where the dashing road agent and his men periodically gather at their outlying camp, sweep down upon the town to strike a blow for justice, and then retire again to their mountain stronghold. Since the locus of good and evil forces varies in other dime novels, however, it would seem that the two poles of the standardized landscape--the town and the outlying camp--have no fixed, intrinsic meaning. Rather, the two areas are essentially neutral in moral value until they are inhabited by a hero or a villain, at which time they become, like the opponents' corners in a boxing ring, places of refuge to which the combatants retire between confrontations. What does not change from story to story, though, is the vast intermediate region of open space: conflicts between the opposing forces may occur anywhere, and the reader must retain an unimpeded view of the pattern of action as it moves swiftly back and forth among the three areas of the standardized landscape.

Yet the open space so important to the Western's setting also creates at least two artistic problems. First of all, since the setting itself is so extensive, it would seem highly implausible for tiny bands of men roaming over the vast prairie to meet very often; hence some motivation short of random chance is necessary to bring opposing parties into conflict, thus insuring plot action. To avoid this problem, dime novelists customarily depict conflicts--especially the climactic, decisive battles which generally end the stories--as organized assaults upon either the town or the outlying camp. For the sake of variety, however, they occasionally stage skirmishes on the intermediate landscape of the open prairie. When they do, conflicts usually take place at a waterhole, a *motte,* or a box canyon where opposing groups are likely to meet, and where the action may be enclosed and intensified.

A second problem related to the setting's open space, however, is more difficult to remedy. Since conflicts involving different groups may and do occur simultaneously on widely scattered areas of the landscape, some device is necessary to unify the overall pattern of action. This problem perhaps explains dime novelists' exclusive use of the unlimited omniscient point of view; by rapidly shifting scenes, authors may narrate events taking place at the same moment on various parts of the landscape. Moreover, as a device analogous to the cinematic technique known as crosscutting, such rapid scene-shifting serves to heighten tension and suspense.

It is not uncommon, though, to find dime novelists resorting to more ingenious techniques. For instance, in *Big Foot Wallace, the King of the Lariat; or, Wild Wolf, the Waco,* Major Sam S. Hall uses the moon as a device to unify a story involving no less than six different parties rapidly approaching each other on the darkened prairie:

> The moon, although still shining brightly, was now low in the western sky, casting its brilliant rays aslant, its arrows kissing alike the paint-daubed cheek of the Commanche [sic], the yellow face of the Mexican, the bronzed features of the

Texan outlaw, and the pallid lily skin of the trembling captive in the Commanche [sic] camp.

Out upon the northwest plain, hidden by a bend of the San Miguel, the orb of night shone down upon a galloping mass of Waco warriors....

On the south bank of the San Miguel, the moon smiled placidly also upon three men, who were driving the cruel spur at every bound of their steeds, as their eyes stared fixedly and painfully ahead....

A similar device appears in Frederick Whittaker's *Top Notch Tom, the Cowboy Outlaw; or, The Satanstown Election,* where a rotating telescope mounted in the belvedere of an isolated ranch house provides the narrator a means of describing, with tactical precision, skirmishes occurring within a radius of six miles. Though admittedly contrived, such unifying devices enable dime novelists to turn problems created by open space to their advantage. As a result, the dime novel–like the modern Western film–occasionally captures the epic power of the West in grand, panoramic scenes in which small parties of horsemen, dwarfed by the boundless, sun-drenched landscape, clash silently in the distance.

Scenes such as this, of course, distill the powerful emotional and psychological appeal that the western landscape is capable of exerting. Balzac, extolling the powerful appeal of the landscape in Cooper's novels, explains that "You incarnate yourself in the country; it passes into you, or you into it," and "you feel it impossible to separate the soil, the vegetation, the waters, their expanse, their configuration, from the interests that agitate you."[3] Dime novelists seldom challenge Cooper's descriptive powers, but they do occasionally succeed in capturing the stirring, oddly mixed feelings of exhilaration and loneliness that the expanse and solitude of the western landscape elicit. "In the midst of the ocean, tossed upon a spar," observes Edward Ellis in *Irona; or, Life on the Old South-West Border,*

> the shipwrecked mariner gains some idea of the vastness of the expanse around him, and of his own littleness in this great world of ours. So the traveler journeying alone over the western prairie, feels, perhaps in a lesser degree, the mighty extent of the American continent. Hour after hour, day after day, he may gallop over the monotonous waves of land; week after week he may kindle his camp-fire on the banks of streams and on the plains themselves, and for months he may wander whither his fancy leads him, without meeting one of his own kind.

Through such descriptions of the measureless vistas of the western landscape, readers of the dime novel–particularly city dwellers–perhaps transcended their twilight existences, satisfying for a moment their longing for unrestricted freedom and primitive, uncomplicated contact with Nature. To them, even what one dime novelist called the "immense, crushing loneliness" of the western landscape was no doubt ennobling and soul-stirring. " 'How beautiful all this is,' " says Frank Weston, pausing to contemplate the vast nothingness of the Texas prairie in *The Mustang-Hunters; or, The Beautiful*

Amazon of the Hidden Valley. " 'It ar' that,' " his rustic companion answers. " 'Give me a hunter's life afore all the sprees and drinks of the settlements. Ef it weren't for my trips to the settlements, I'd never be onhappy.' "

STRUCTURE AND PLOT

If one were to apply to the dime novel Cooper's familiar dictum that "On the human imagination, events produce the effects of time," one might expect all of history to pass before one's eyes in a single dime novel, for events in these early Westerns scarcely allow a reader time to catch his breath. In *Buffalo Bill's Leap for Life; or, The White Death of Beaver Wash,* for example, the extraordinary plainsman escapes from a fort attacked by a thousand Indians, fights two jaguars and a grizzly bear, survives a powerful explosion, and emerges unscathed from a second Indian attack—all within a span of four pages. Though more exaggerated than most, this story is not entirely atypical. Often the plot of the dime novel seems nothing more than a fast-paced, loosely-connected sequence of fistfights, gunplay, and hairbreadth escapes strung out interminably and tied together by a happy ending. Certainly the typical plot of the dime novel is both implausible and complicated. Yet through this labyrinth of complications, discoveries, and improbable reversals winds the unifying thread of myth.

In its fundamental conflicts, its dialectical form, and its recurrent plot situations and motifs, the Western embodies the universal pattern of human experience that Northrop Frye has labeled the *mythos* of romance. Hence several of the characteristic features of romance are worth recalling. Essentially, Frye explains, the romance is a collective oedipal fantasy, the "nearest of all literary forms to the wish fulfilment dream...." But in addition to its psychological dimension, the romance also possesses a related social dimension: the romance reflects and embodies humanity's perpetual "search for some kind of imaginative golden age in time or space." This search takes the form of a quest undertaken by a central character in pursuit of an ideal. In English literature, the quest romance is best illustrated by the first book of *The Faerie Queene,* in which St. George undertakes a mission to slay the dragon and thereby "raise Eden in the wilderness and restore England to the status of Eden." Moreover, Frye continues, since the romantic quest leads the hero through a sequence of minor and major adventures, the "essential element of plot in romance is adventure...." This plot normally has three stages: "the stage of the perilous journey and the preliminary minor adventures; the crucial struggle, usually some kind of a battle in which either the hero or his foe, or both, must die; and the exaltation of the hero." If successful in his quest, the hero is hailed as "a redeemer of society," and--provided he survives the quest--his reward generally includes a maiden whom he has "rescued from the unwelcome embraces of another" or "from giants or bandits," and whom he often takes as his bride.[1]

Frye's discussion of the *mythos* of romance provides a useful framework in which to examine the basic narrative structure of the popular Western, for the dime Western is essentially a nineteenth century American adaptation of the traditional romance.[2] Each of the characteristic features of the romance recurs in the dime novel Western, but each has been influenced by cultural dynamics and transformed accordingly. Like the traditional romance, which gives literary form to humanity's "search for some kind of imaginative golden age in time or space," the dime novel Western functions as an elaborate social ritual which embodies and affirms nineteenth century America's search for a utopian society of comfort, happiness, and equality. This ideal society, implicit in the Western's frontier setting and suggested by Edenic imagery, synthesizes the respective values of wilderness and civilization while transcending the limitations of each.

Understood within this context, the Western may be viewed as a narrative construct whose unifying principle is the Western hero's quest to reorder reality in terms of his own vision of the ideal world. Since the questing hero naturally encounters obstacles which he must confront and overcome, the essential element of plot in the Western–like that of the traditional romance–is adventure. In the dime novel this adventure usually derives from a recurrent pattern of capture, flight, and pursuit–a plot pattern whose origins lie in both religious and secular versions of the Indian captivity narrative, as well as popular melodrama.[3] The narrative structure of the Western further resembles that of the traditional romance insofar as its plot is tripartite. The titular hero of *Seth Jones: or, The Captives of the Frontier,* for example, first undertakes a perilous journey through the forest in an attempt to rescue a maiden in distress from the clutches of the cruel Mohawks. Seth's early efforts prove fruitless, but eventually he and his stalwart companions engage the savages in a crucial struggle which corresponds to the second stage of the archetypal romantic plot. Emerging from the struggle victorious, Seth escorts the maiden back to her grieving family in the settlement. Shortly thereafter, in the third and final stage of the plot, Seth flings off the humble backwoods garb in which he has been disguised and stands revealed as the maiden's long-lost, genteel suitor. Handsome, resplendent in his gentlemanly attire, the beaming hero wins the plaudits of the surprised and grateful family. Disclaiming the family's stunned pronouncement that he must have "risen from the dead," the exalted hero leads his eager sweetheart to the altar.

As the unifying principle of the Western's narrative pattern, the hero's quest to reorder reality in terms of his personal vision of an ideal world becomes the axis of the Western's moral structure. Clustered around this axis is a complex of minor characters whose moral support or opposition constitutes the principal source of plot conflicts. Discussing this aspect of the *mythos* of romance, Frye observes that "Characters tend to be either for or against the quest. If they assist it they are idealized as simply gallant or pure; if they obstruct it they are caricatured as simply villainous or cowardly. Hence every typical character in romance tends to have his moral opposite confronting him...." These pairs of moral opposites, Frye explains, include the hero and the villain, the heroine and the siren or dark temptress, the hero's faithful companion and the traitor, and animals friendly to the hero and animals unfriendly to the hero. There are, in addition, two archetypal characters whose respective relationships to the antithetical moral scheme of the romance are somewhat anomalous: the child of Nature, such as the shy and elusive, half-wild forest nymph, who is generally a friend or servant of the hero; and, the rustic clown who is "licensed to show fear or make realistic comments," and who provides "a localized safety valve for realism without allowing it to disrupt the conventions of romance."[4] Each of the typical characters of the romance has his counterpart in the dime novel Western. In most instances, plot conflict in the dime novel arises from the confrontation of these paired moral opposites.

The Western's principal antagonists are the hero and villain. Generally, the hero himself is the personification of the ideal he seeks. In him the conflict between wilderness and civilization is internalized and resolved; his character synthesizes cherished values associated with wilderness and civilization respectively, and therefore images the utopian society of the future. Consequently, his value system and conception of the utopian ideal closely correspond to those of the ordinary reader, and thus dictate the ethical system which prevails within the fictive world of the narrative. With this ethical system the villain is at odds. For though the villain is the hero's virtual equal in power and skill, he possesses a world view alien to that of the hero and the reader. Conflict results when the hero and the villain meet, each acting out of a desire for unrestricted power to assert his individual will in an attempt to reorder reality in terms of his own vision of the ideal world.

Villains of several types appear in the dime novel. In the early dime novel the villain is often an Indian who envisions the ideal world as an untrammeled state of Nature, a virtual happy hunting ground where the white man never ventures. Though understandable–and even noble when abstracted from the novel and viewed in its own right–this vision is incompatible with the hero's utopian ideal. Hence the Indian is both an obstacle in the path of the questing hero and a real and imminent threat to the advance of civilization toward the utopian society of the future. As a result, the dime novel Indian is most often a cunning and brutal, innately evil savage. Wontum, for example, the principal villain of *Quindaro; or, The Heroine of Fort Laramie,* has a "brow black as midnight" and "snake-like eyes," and several times he is called "The Evil One." A similar character, Telonga, appears in *Queen of the Woods; or, The Shawnee Captive.* Believing that the Great Spirit intends Kentucky to remain forever a hunting ground for the Shawnee, Telonga leads his "painted rascals" against the encroaching white settlers until, mortally wounded in combat with the novel's hero, he utters the conventional *ubi sunt* and dies with a final cry of sorrow, "My people–my people!"

THE DEADWOOD DICK LIBRARY

Copyrighted by JAMES SULLIVAN

Copyright 1880-1886, by Beadle & Adams. Entered at Post Office, New York, N. Y., as second class matter. Mar. 15, 1899.

No. 34   THE ARTHUR WESTBROOK CO.
Cleveland, Ohio   Vol. III

"BACK, FRANK FOSTER," PERCIVAL ORDERED, "OR I'LL FINISH THE JOB DEADWOOD DICK LEFT UNFINISHED, UP IN THE MINES."

Another character in this same novel, Simon Girty, typifies a second type of villain who often appears in the dime novel–the half-breed or white renegade. As commonly portrayed, he is the exact moral opposite of the hero. Whereas the hero is the embodiment of the best of both worlds–wilderness and civilization, Indian freedom and white society–the renegade or half-breed unites, in the words of one dime novelist, "the worst passions of both races, without the slightest of their virtues." The renegade's vision of the ideal world is both narrow and egoistic, lacking even the noble motive of racial pride that accounts for the villainous Indian's concept of the ideal world. In the renegade the quest for a better world has degenerated to an all-consuming lust for power and wealth.

This selfish motive also directs the actions of a third incarnation of the Western villain, the crafty plutocrat who opposes the hero in dime novels written during the 1870s and afterward. Villains of this type are the exponents of unpopular economic, social, political or legal institutions whose malpractices and inequities they clearly personify; they are bankers, land speculators, capitalists, politicians, lawyers, and even, like the notorious Jack Sin of the Diamond Dick novels, sheriffs. Employing their wealth and positions of authority to further their own interests at the expense of the uninformed majority, villains of this ilk represent perhaps the most insidious threat to the realization of the ideal society.

Plot conflict in the dime novel also results from the moral opposition of the heroine and the siren. In the vast majority of dime novels the heroine is pure and unassailably virtuous–traits which establish her kinship to that sisterhood of innocent heroines who traditionally function in the sentimental novel and other popular arts as guardians of conventional morality. Angelic in appearance and shy in demeanor, the dime novel heroine is equally devoted to both God and the hero, on whom she bestows her fervent but wholly ethereal adoration. She is also associated with wisdom, power, and wealth. Often she stands in a position to inherit a fortune from her powerful and prestigious father or uncle. Minnie Potter, the heroine of *The James Boys in No Man's Land; or, The Bandit King's Last Ride,* is "a gold mine," and at the end of the tale she inherits a million dollars. Similarly, the wealthy heroine of *The Pirate of the Placers; or, Joaquin's Death-Hunt* is named, significantly enough, Lota Sylva. As a symbol of power and wealth, the heroine commands the attentions of both villain and hero alike, and usually she is a mere pawn captured by the villain and rescued by the hero. Whoever wins her, of course, will acquire the power and wealth necessary to reorder the world in accord with his own personal vision of the ideal. As a result, the heroine is symbolically identified with the ideal. In the majority of Westerns–and always in the maturation story, where the hero is an impetuous eastern tenderfoot- -the heroine personifies the ideal society that the hero seeks to realize. Any threat to the heroine, especially an assault upon her virtue, constitutes a threat to the integrity of the utopian ideal. Thus, in his efforts to foil the villain's repeated attempts to seduce the heroine, the hero is not merely proving himself worthy of the heroine's love; he is undergoing a series of learning experiences and trials through which he acquires and demonstrates his ability to protect the ideal from corruption and to preserve the possibility of realizing the utopian society of the future. Indeed, the hero is himself becoming a nearer approximation of the ideal; he is abandoning false values and acquiring instead the true values which alone can insure the realization of the ideal. The hero's eventual marriage to the heroine thus symbolically corroborates the hero's exaltation and his attainment of the ideal. In other Westerns, however–that is, in stories of romantic synthesis, such as *The Virginian,* where the hero is an experienced Westerner–the heroine comes from the East and personifies civilization. Hence the marriage of the western male to the eastern female symbolizes the synthesis of the respective values of wilderness and civilization. In this case the hero and heroine together represent the utopian ideal.

Although the heroine ultimately wins the affections of the hero, she faces a potent rival in the form of a dark and alluring woman of mystery who, tempting the hero away from the path of virtue, constitutes an implicit threat to the successful completion of the quest. Dime novelists frequently portray the temptress as a fiery and passionate woman of Latin blood. Possessing raven hair and a lustrous olive complexion, she is easily recognizable as the moral opposite of the blonde and fair-skinned heroine. If the temptress is not a Latin, she is likely to be of mixed blood. Like Cherokee Sue, whose beauty rivals that of blonde and blue-eyed Alice LaRue, the "lily of the forest," in Edward L. Wheeler's *Wild Ivan, The Boy Claude Duval,* the temptress may be a half-breed. Or, like Conchita, the dark lady of Wheeler's *Apollo Bill, the Trail Tornade; or, Rowdy Kate from Right-Bower,* she may even be a half-breed with a Spanish name. In any event, the temptress is usually an active sexual aggressor whose fits of jealous fury contrast vividly with the bland and even-tempered behavior of the passive heroine. The temptress is thus a dangerous companion. When the hero spurns her affections-- as he invariably does--she joins forces with the villain and plots the hero's downfall. Eventually, however, she discovers that the villain, too, secretly despises her, and that he is merely using her as a tool. She then vents her violence upon him. In the end she either dies by the villain's hand or her own, or else she endures a living death as a fallen woman.

Although major plot conflicts in the dime novel arise from the moral antagonism between hero and villain, heroine and temptress, minor conflicts arise from confrontations between the hero's faithful companion and *his* moral opposite, the traitor in league with the villain. Repeatedly rescuing the hero from tight spots, the hero's sidekick also exposes the traitor's covert attempts to subvert the quest. In the typical situation, the sidekick confronts the traitor openly, often in a crowded saloon or on the open prairie. The traitor, however, is a sly, cowardly figure who lacks even that strength which is the villain's sole compelling trait. The traitor shrinks from open confrontation, preferring instead to lurk in shadows or to lie in the safety of ambush. The conflict between the hero's sidekick and the skulking traitor precipitates violence, and often leads to the involvement of the hero. Normally, a gruesome death awaits the traitor.

The Western, like the traditional romance, also accords a central role to animals. They, too, may hinder or help the hero's quest. Minor plot incidents often involve the hero's struggle with a ferocious beast of the forest, usually a mountain lion or a grizzly bear. Though these confrontations hinder the quest, the hero sometimes anticipates them eagerly, regarding them as opportunities to measure his prowess. When Davy Crockett spots bear tracks in *The Bear-Hunter; or, Davy Crockett as a Spy,* he is "nerved by hopes of meeting with his favorite game.... The unusual length of the claws, foot, stride, etc., filled Crockett with hope that the bear was a grizzly; a species with which he had never yet measured his prowess, though long anxious for the opportunity."

Figuring even more prominently in the Western plot are those animals friendly to the hero. In the early dime novel, where the hero is a trapper or hunter, he is generally accompanied by a dog. Such dogs–usually resembling Hector, Natty Bumppo's toothless hound, or Peter, the talented dog of *Nick of the Woods*–aid the questing hero by tracking down antagonists. Chaw, Shank Shingle's loyal canine in *Daniel Boone's Best Shot; or The Perils of the Kentucky Pioneers,* is the "best dorge for b'ars an' Injuns ever knowed. He can smell 'um for a mile, an' is sure death when he lays a hold...." In the later dime novel, where the hero is a plainsman, cowboy, or outlaw, his dog is replaced by a horse. Famous horses introduced in the dime novel include Buffalo Bill's incomparable mount Powder Face, who often lies down in the tall prairie grass to hide his master from Indians, and Jesse James' "midnight steed" Sirocco. This trend continues today, of course, in the television Western, where such celebrated equine twosomes as Silver and Scout or Trigger and Buttermilk risk their lives for no more reward than an occasional sugar cube. Primarily, horses support the quest by providing the hero transportation, but they may also be counted upon to aid the hero in difficult moments. Possible plot situations are virtually endless: when the hero is asleep and unaware of approaching danger, his horse neighs a warning; when the hero is knocked unconscious, his horse nuzzles him back to his senses; and when the hero is tied up, his horse gnaws through the ropes or gallops back to town where, riderless, he attracts the attention of a rescue party.

The Western plot also makes use of those traditional minor characters of romance who, though morally neutral children of Nature, may nevertheless be brought to serve the hero. Like Telie Doe of *Nick of the Woods,* these Nature sprites usually appear in the dime novel as forest maidens of mysterious origin. They sometimes function as messengers, often warning of impending danger, but their rapport with Nature makes them especially valuable as guides. In "Red Arrow, the Wolf Demon; or, The Queen of the Kanawha," a story released in Beadle's *Saturday Journal,* the hero is guided by Kanawha Kate, a shy and beautiful huntress to whom "the forest-although to strange eyes a trackless wilderness-was as familiar as her own little garden. She knew the way as well in the darkness as in the light. She was, in very truth, a child of the wilderness, and from infancy she had traversed freely the brown paths of the wild woods." Children of Nature in the dime Western are exclusively female. Male characters who might be expected to fill this role–the noble savage, for instance–function as the hero's faithful companion.

One other minor character figures in the plot of the dime novel, though with less frequency than most. He is the rustic clown of the traditional romance–a character who, according to Frye, calls "attention to realistic aspects of life, like fear in the presence of danger, which threaten the unity of the romantic mood." Psychologically, the clown provides "a localized safety valve for realism without allowing it to disrupt the conventions of romance."[5] This character appears most notably in *Daniel Boone's Best Shot; or, The Perils of the Kentucky Pioneers,* where aptly named Bill Whiner is a habitual "croaker of evil." Each time Boone's party prepares to attack a band of Indians, Whiner's face assumes a "funereal" expression. Repeatedly he urges retreat, vociferously predicting that the entire party will be "filled full of arrows and scalped before daylight." Always, however, the withering stares of his companions silence him, and when the battle commences he rises to the occasion and fights as gallantly as anyone else. And naturally, when the battle ends in victory, Whiner calmly announces that he was never really worried at all.

Given this imposing array of characters who aid or oppose the quest, a virtually unlimited variety of plot situations and minor conflicts is possible. It is important to recognize, however, that while the formal, abstract structure of the *mythos* of romance–its central narrative pattern of the quest, its pairing of moral antagonists–is unchanging and universal, the plot actions permitted within this structure are various, and their symbolic content is culturally specific. Within its universal narrative structure the Western incorporates a variety of topical conflicts—e.g. civilization versus wilderness, social progress versus individual freedom, law versus morality-which wax or wane in significance in relation to the dominant cultural pressures of a given era. Between 1860 and 1900 two basic plots predominated in the dime novel Western. Although the quest for an ideal world is implicit in the overall structure of both of these plots, both likewise demonstrate an overriding concern with one or more specific cultural conflicts experienced during the last half of the nineteenth century.

Dime novels written prior to 1875 were most commonly maturation stories that fused the sentimental novel's triangular love plot with fast-paced western adventure. J.R. Scott's *Red River Bill, the Prince of Scouts* illustrates the pattern of action common to the maturation story. The tale concerns Harold Tracy, a young eastern tenderfoot who, in company with veteran scouts Red River Bill and Nick Spooner, journeys through the wilderness in a perilous attempt to rescue the novel's heroine, Anna Adams, from a Sioux war party led by the notorious renegade Burling Sharp. Although Harold's intentions are noble, his misconceptions about wilderness life have dire consequences; again and again he makes near-fatal mistakes which jeopardize the lives of his companions. Gradually, however, he abandons his initial misconceptions, and when Bill and Nick fall into the hands of the savages Harold realizes that the fate of the captives rests entirely in his hands. In the end, Harold redeems himself: killing Burling Sharp, he rescues the captives and thereby endears himself to Anna. She, we are told, "believed he had proved himself a man in the true sense of the word, and she afterwards became his wife."

The love story which unfolds in *Red River Bill* departs only slightly from the triangular love plot in its classic form. Readers familiar with the sentimental novel will recognize the characteristic struggle between bitter rivals for the hand of an innocent heroine. One of the rivals, the hero, is a paragon of virtue who offers the heroine pure romantic love; the other rival is a villain who sometimes feigns romantic love but who in all cases acts solely out of lust and greed. When the heroine declares her preference for the hero, the villain abducts her and menaces her with "a fate worse than death." The hero then kills the villain, rescues the heroine, and all ends happily amid the sonorous clangor of wedding bells. In *Red River Bill,* and indeed in most early Westerns, the love plot commences when the villain abducts the heroine, thereby initiating a sequence of capture, pursuit, and eventual escape.

Reduced to its essentials, the triangular love plot allegorizes the triumph of good over evil. The plot assumes a broader dimension, however, when incorporated in the Western maturation story, where it functions as a means of working out the dilemma posed by civilization's confrontation with the wilderness. Ostensibly, the heroine represents the ideal society that the young and impetuous hero, a representative of contemporary civilization, seeks to realize. The villain, who in these early novels is nearly always an Indian or white renegade, represents the savagery and unprincipled self-interest which life in the wilderness permits, and which pose a threat to the ideal society popularly envisioned. To be sure, the villain does not manifest the values which will usher in the utopian future. But neither does the immature hero; his overconfidence and deficiency in wilderness skills are the earmarks of his lack of restraint and self-sufficiency, important attributes without which civilization cannot safely assimilate the dangerous freedom and absence of institutional controls concomitant with wilderness life. Not until the hero has acquired these mature attributes from the elderly veterans who accompany him is he worthy of attaining the ideal he seeks, a union which his marriage to the undefiled heroine presumably symbolizes. And since the hero's exaltation and marriage follow his elimination of the villain and his assimilation of the values personified by the veteran woodsmen, the overall plot projects a resolution of the conflict between civilization and wilderness. A utopian society, the plot suggests, will develop through a gradual process of maturation, of synthesis and mutual refinement, in which society will overcome the pernicious influences associated with wilderness life while at the same time assimilating the positive influences associated with life in a state of Nature. This is, of course, the kind of plot one might expect to find in dime Westerns penned during the 1860s and early 1870s.

The plots of dime novels written after 1875, however, reflect the more primitivistic posture likewise evident in the development during this period of a more rebellious hero and a standardized setting designed to facilitate the expression of social criticism. Again, novels of this era use the triangular love plot to allegorize the realization of a utopian society, but the plot's earlier emphasis on the problems of assimilating the wilderness yields to a more pronounced emphasis on oppression of the weak by the strong. In almost all cases this oppression takes the form of economic or sexual exploitation.

The conventional plot appears in *Buffalo Bill, the Buckskin King; or, The Amazon of the West,* a story penned by Prentiss Ingraham under the pseudonym Major Dangerfield Burr, and released in 1880. The story begins as Lord Varian Elphistone, an English nobleman, arrives in America and engages the services of Buffalo Bill to investigate the suspicious circumstances surrounding the death of Lord Varian's elder brother. Events soon reveal that the villain responsible for the murder is Royal Keene, a card-sharp, womanizer, and all around ne'r-do-well who spends much of his time leading a band of shifty-eyed felons known as the Nighthawks. In the process of trailing Keene around the countryside, Buffalo Bill stumbles upon Keene's plot to marry his beautiful cousin Louise Melville and to bilk her wealthy father of a gold mine. In league with Royal Keene is an assortment of other miscreants, most notably Moses Moloch, a banker and speculator "who had won the title of *millionaire* by taking advantage of the adversity of others," and his pompous cohort Judge Shyster, a self-styled "luminary and pleader at the bar." Buffalo Bill's efforts to upset the conspiracy involve him in a series of gunfights, duels, snares and escapes. Whenever he is in a tight spot,

Buffalo Bill receives assistance from two women devoted to his interests: Star Eye, a Pawnee princess whose superb tracking ability and mastery of "prairie craft" prove invaluable; and Wild Nell, a mysterious she-devil whose prospects in life have been ruined by the former attentions of Royal Keene. When Keene kidnaps Louise, who fears the meaning behind the villain's smoldering leers, Buffalo Bill gathers around him a band of loyal followers and storms the Nighthawk stronghold in the mountains. The dashing plainsman then slays Keene in a duel with knives, and frees Louise, but while he is thus occupied Moses Moloch and Judge Shyster escape to St. Louis, presumably to hatch another wicked plot in a sequel. Ingraham then ties up the novel's loose ends in a brief synopsis chapter: Lord Varian returns to England and marries his sweetheart; Star Eye becomes the "squaw wife" of a noble young man who has played only a minor role in the tale; and Wild Nell, a "wreck of womanhood," goes on to live a lonely life in a humble cabin apart from the world. In an odd departure from the customary plot, the story concludes with the implication that Buffalo Bill will eventually marry Louise Melville. Here, though, as in one or two other Buffalo Bill novels in which the prince of plainsmen is permitted not only to rescue the heroine but to marry her, Ingraham seems merely to be accounting for Cody's actual marriage to Louisa Frederici.

As this tale suggests, the plot of the later dime novel features a strong and independent hero who, if he is a plainsman like Buffalo Bill or Young Wild West, roves around the countryside seeking adventure. Coming upon trouble, he intercedes on behalf of the weak or defenseless party, generally a young woman and her aged, sick, or lunatic father. Occasionally the hero comes to the aid of a young man whose sister or female cousin serves to introduce the love interest. In initial encounters the hero matches his strength against Indians or uncouth ruffians, but he soon learns that such second-rate desperadoes are merely the agents of a master villain. Commonly a banker, lawyer, or politician, the villain conspires to abduct the heroine and to defraud her wealthy father. When the hero intercedes, he is usually captured and held prisoner. But with the aid of the sidekick who often accompanies him, or a woman devoted to his safety–a lovesick Indian girl, say, or a mysterious woman with a tainted past–the hero escapes. Eventually he confronts the villain in a fair fight, slays him, and frees the heroine and her father from further danger, whereupon the heroine and an assortment of unmarried couples marry and live happily ever after. This overall plot pattern seldom changes significantly, though several variants may occur. In most cowboy novels (excluding the Buck Taylor stories and the later Ted Strong stories), the hero does not rove around the countryside; instead he resides in a fixed locale–for instance, the Black Mountain Ranch in the early Ted Strong stories–where trouble comes to him. Another variant occurs in outlaw stories, where the hero himself is the victim of oppression and injustice. This, of course, complicates his efforts to aid others in distress.

In any of its common variations, however, the basic plot of the later dime novel allegorizes the role of individual strength and virtue in maintaining personal freedoms and eradicating from existing society all forms of injustice and immorality which impede society's progress toward the utopian ideal. Insofar as the plot ends with the rescue and marriage of the undefiled heroine, the later dime novel projects the same utopian future idealized in the earlier maturation story. Yet the emphasis is no longer directed at society's confrontation with the wilderness; rather, the emphasis falls on society's internal conflicts. What these conflicts are is not difficult to discern. The villains are wealthy capitalists who exploit the common man: bankers who thrive on others' adversity and who appropriate personal fortunes; politicians who make a mockery of the democratic process; lawyers who manipulate the law for personal gain. Nor is it difficult to discern the message implicit in the resolution of these conflicts. Poor, disenfranchised, bound by laws which limit freedom rather than protecting it, the common man must stand up for his rights. He must overcome his ignorance and apathy. And he must rally behind those strongwilled individuals who refuse to be exploited, who will not surrender their rights or stand by idly while others are inveigled to do so. In an age of increasing class strife and labor unrest, this message no doubt struck a responsive chord.

Yet the exploitation represented in the dime novel is not exclusively economic; it is also sexual. Two of the more intriguing aspects of the triangular love plot are its reliance upon a sexual symbolic framework and its customary association of sexual transgression and death. Neither of these characteristics, of course, is peculiar to the dime novel. Endlessly retelling the *Genesis* account of the Fall, sentimental novels of the eighteenth and early nineteenth centuries had firmly established the villain as a specifically sexual symbol of universal evil. By attempting to seduce the heroine, he sought to overcome the power of good in the world, and for his efforts he was ultimately destroyed. Likewise, the heroine who allowed herself to be seduced inevitably died, usually in childbirth or simply by wasting away under the pangs of an unbearable guilt. Heroines were spotlessly innocent; if they were anything less they received the "wages of sin."

It is not surprising that popular American fiction of the eighteenth and nineteenth centuries betrayed a penchant for associating sexual transgression and death.[6] In a Christian society that had traditionally regarded primordial sin as sexual sin, the association of sexual transgression and death was not an unnatural reaction. Had not Eve succumbed? And had not mankind been punished with pain and death? Literature that implied a connection between sexual misconduct and death thus served a didactic purpose: it sternly warned of the dangers of sexual license. Seducers, such literature taught, died violently, and fallen women were deserted and left to bear the physical and spiritual consequences alone. Sexual sin was the ultimate sin; it would therefore invoke the ultimate punishment—death and damnation.

Always an important plot element, the wages of sin motif played an increasingly significant role in popular fiction written during the last half of the nineteenth century. As early as the 1840s, the moral ramifications of industrialization and urbanization were becoming painfully evident. "The inordinate pursuit of money," declared

Reverend Caleb Stetson in 1842, "for the gratification of avarice, vanity, pride, and ambition, has deeply corrupted the principles of the country...." This is "the age of gaudy wealth," said an Episcopal Bishop in the 1850s. "Wealth came in and created social distinction which took the place of family, and thus society became vulgarized."[7] Yet it was not only the clergy that noted the moral decline of the nation. Even *The American Review,* a Whig journal normally sympathetic to commercial enterprise, observed in 1845 that the nation's commitment to material progress was occasioning "an excessive barrenness of real moral excellencies."[8]

One of the more disturbing repercussions of the economic revolution was its effect upon woman's traditional role as a symbol of innocence and moral rectitude. Economic necessity was more and more frequently causing the American woman to forsake her time honored place in the home, and to assume a position in the national economy. Many people regarded this trend as a threat to woman's morality and, consequently, to the sanctity of the home, the institution of marriage, and the preservation of the family unit. In the home, woman was isolated from the temptations of the outside world; her virtue was safe from assault. In the working world, however, she was vulnerable; she might even assume traditional male prerogatives, including sexual license. Such fears were not without some foundation in fact. As early as 1833, a New York doctor alarmed by the city's growing number of prostitutes reported that he could cite *"many instances of young and even middle-aged women, who have been 'lost to virtue', apparently by no other cause than the lowness of wages* and THE ABSOLUTE IMPOSSIBILITY OF PROCURING THE NECESSARIES OF LIFE BY HONEST INDUSTRY."[9] By 1893, when Stephen Crane's *Maggie: A Girl of the Streets* chronicled the misfortunes of a young woman on her own in the sordid metropolis, the story of the innocent girl gone wrong had become disturbingly familiar to the American public.

The dime novel Western responded to popular fears about the declining morality of women. Through the pattern of action embodied in the triangular love plot the dime novel rigidified the standards of female characters, punished sexual transgression, and reaffirmed the sanctity of marriage. Without fail, the villain died violently and the fallen woman earned the wages of sin. Unlike her counterpart in the sentimental novel, however, the fallen woman of the dime novel did not suffer a fate so colorless and jejune as death by childbirth or guilt; instead, her penance was sensational and violent. She became either a revenge-crazed tigress who first killed her seducer and then herself, or a bitter Amazon who, stripped of her femininity, endured a kind of living death.

Both varieties of ruined women appear in Edward L. Wheeler's *The Black Hills Jezebel; or, Deadwood Dick's Ward,* a story which clearly illustrates the use of the wages of sin motif in the dime novel plot. Wheeler opens the tale by introducing Girard Athol and his daughter Kate. Girard, a cripple, is searching for his wife, Kate's mother, who years before had married him for his money and subsequently departed with his gold savings. Girard has learned, however, that his unfaithful wife is now living somewhere in the Black Hills and calling herself Madame Cheviot, for she has illegally remarried and plans to marry yet a third time in the near future. Crazed by jealousy and a desire for revenge, the wronged husband resolves to prevent the forthcoming marriage at all costs.

Like her hunchbacked father, Kate seems at first an unorthodox character. She wears men's clothes, handles ruffians with ease, and goes by the alliterating nickname "Kentucky Kit," a standard attribute of male characters in the dime novel. As her lack of femininity suggests, she is a fallen woman: her father describes her as a genuine "blue-grass widow," and Ned Harris, better known as Deadwood Dick, can see that the lady has a "secret under all her bright and shining exterior." Moreover, unlike the typically shy and submissive heroines of the dime novel, Kate is decidedly bold. Discovering Deadwood Dick asleep in the grass, she steals a kiss, thinking, "I'll bet he's a reg'lar 'masher,' too, as they say out East. Anyhow, it wouldn't take long for him to 'mash' me, if he's as good as he looks." When the noble outlaw awakes, Kate disregards his "bold, unwavering eye" and declares that she trusts him, "though you are the first I have placed confidence in, for many a year."

In the meantime, the evil Madame Cheviot has learned of the proximity of Girard Athol and Kentucky Kit, and consequently she hires Bloody Bill and Black Bob to dispose of them--along with the ever dangerous Deadwood Dick. The two ruffians bungle the scheme, however, and during the wedding ceremony between Madame Cheviot and a wealthy rancher, Kentucky Kit unexpectedly arrives and shoots her mother. But the wicked woman is only wounded, and she attempts to conduct the wedding again several days later. This time her hunchbacked husband arrives on the scene. Bringing the ceremony to a standstill, Girard Athol shouts, "my time has come for vengeance. It is too late to mend your ways, for Jezebel! you shall die ere you do any further deviltry." And with a demonic laugh, the betrayed husband plunges a dagger into his faithless wife and escapes.

While this main plot is unfolding, a sub-plot relates the fortunes of another fallen woman. Millicent Raymond, who has been seduced by the villainous Ralph Randall, begs him to fulfill his promise to marry her: "What assurance have I that you will fulfill your promise, to me, sir, after dyeing my soul, with sin, to satisfy your will?" Randall replies that he will indeed marry her, but only if she will consent to rob her father and murder Deadwood Dick. Reluctantly, she agrees to comply with his demand, for presumably she is pregnant and would rather face "the inevitable result of a few months to come" with a husband. Yet she also issues Randall a stern warning: "...if you refuse to marry me, I'll send you to one of the most horrible deaths that my ingenuity can devise. You shall find that Millicent Raymond is yet able to right her wrongs, or to kill her betrayer and avenge them." Shortly thereafter, Randall betrays signs of growing affection for Kentucky Kit, and Millicent responds instantly. She kills Kentucky Kit and then herself. Randall manages to survive the events of the novel, but only because he must live on to act villainously in a sequel.

As this outline suggests, the plot of the dime

novel Western characteristically reaffirms the Biblical admonition that "the wages of sin is death." Girard Athol kills Madame Cheviot because she has stolen his gold, but clearly her sexual betrayal outweighs her larceny. Hence the deaths of the novel's female characters–Madame Cheviot, Kentucky Kit, and Millicent Raymond–relate directly to sexual misconduct. To the reader disturbed by apparent moral decline, it was no doubt comforting to find his conviction reaffirmed that sin brings punishment and that evil ultimately destroys itself.

The frequency with which dime novelists employed plots based either on maturation, one man's crusade against oppression, or the wages of sin, suggests that these particular narrative sequences recurred in the dime novel because of their peculiar suitability as patterns of action through which to address the unique cultural conflicts and psychological preoccupations of late nineteenth century America. Retaining the timeless, universal structure of the traditional quest romance, the dime Western's conventionalized plots addressed timely issues as well. The maturation stories that abounded in the early dime novel offered readers needed reassurance that America, too, was maturing; that the national character was growing stronger; that society was systematically eradicating evil and marching steadfastly forward toward a utopian future. Similarly, the later dime novel's stories of a strong individual's successful fight against economic and sexual exploitation dramatized the economic and moral problems of the age, glorified individualism, and provided larger-than-life heroes who, leading a wayward society back to the path of righteousness, guided the nation toward its utopian destiny. The triangular love plot that informed the standard plots of both early and later dime novels served a related function; through the wages of sin motif the triangular love plot endorsed conventional moral values and affirmed that virtue would ultimately prevail over evil. Surely, these plots uniformly suggested, a better world is at hand.

BEADLE'S FRONTIER SERIES

No. 60.

TUSCALOOSA SAM

or LIFE IN THE WILDS.

BY W. J. HAMILTON.

THE UNIFYING VISION

After nearly seventy years of furious publication, millions of miles of newsprint, and countless bloody conflicts and hairbreadth escapes, the dime novel died a lingering death in the late 1920s. Several factors contributed to its demise, including prohibitive second-class postal rates and the rising popularity of films.[1] Those publishing houses that did manage to survive, notably Street & Smith and Frank Tousey, did so by gradually altering the standard dime novel format, literally transforming it over a period of years into a pulp magazine. During their heyday in the late twenties and early thirties such popular pulps as *Western Story, Far West,* and *Ranch Romances* sold at the rate of twenty million copies per month. The early years of the century also witnessed the emergence of a new breed of Western writers who added immeasurably to the popular Western canon. Zane Grey and Eugene Manlove Rhodes began publishing shortly after the turn of the century, and subsequent decades brought popularity to Max Brand, Frederick Glidden, and Ernest Haycox, to name only a few.

Today, Westerns appear in various formats, in magazines and books, on movie and television screens, and they continue to be astonishingly popular. Yet the dime novel, so important a medium in the evolution of the Western, has outlived its era and is today consigned to the files of private collectors and the rare book rooms of a handful of major libraries.

No single factor, of course, adequately accounts for the phenomenal popularity that the dime novel Western enjoyed in its time. Undoubtedly, much of its success resulted from its intrinsic entertainment value as an autonomous artistic construct--its unity of setting, character, and action, and its ordered vision of reality. So, too, its popularity no doubt resulted in part from its reliance upon an archetypal structure that reflects and embodies the most fundamental and universal concerns of mankind. Yet both of these factors characterize all popular art forms. Neither distinguishes the Western from any other popular formula, nor does either satisfactorily account for the enduring popularity of the Western *per se.* It seems, rather, that the Western's unique character and its ensuing popularity result largely from factors which are expressly cultural.

The Western evolved as an expression of nineteenth century America's prevailing attitude toward history, progress, and the national destiny. In the early part of the century, apocalyptic visions and physiocratic theories had nurtured a poetic conception of the national destiny based on the conquest of the wilderness and the future foundation of a pastoral utopia in the West. As popularly conceived, this utopia would combine the respective advantages of civilization and wilderness while transcending the disadvantages of each; it would be a land of plenty, of human bliss, of freedom and equality. For this reason Americans revered progress, seeing in the historical process a trend toward the perfection of society and the realization of an ideal world. Yet as the century progressed the utopian vision became increasingly difficult to sustain. Gargantuan economic and social forces associated with the industrial revolution steadily polarized society, corrupted political and social institutions, and precipitated moral decline. Giant corporations swallowed up small businesses, monopolized industry, manipulated Government policy. The public became dependent on trusts like Armour, International Harvester, Weyerhauser, Standard Oil, and United States Steel for its jobs, food, clothing, housing, and transportation. Disputes between capital and labor led to bloody confrontations and paralyzing strikes. Mechanization and the influx of immigrant labor depressed wages, created unemployment, and forced many men and women into crime and vice. Americans in larger and larger numbers soon came to the realization that progress and perfection were not necessarily related. Indeed, as Cooper had predicted long before, the trend of history seemed ominous; instead of improving, the quality of life was perceptibly deteriorating. America's glorious future, once a virtual certainty, was becoming a matter for grave doubt. In the face of growing disillusionment and anxiety, the mass of Americans sought reassurance that the ideal world was still a golden possibility. And in the setting, characters, and plots of the dime novel Western they found this reassurance.

That we are still reluctant today to abandon our vision of an ideal world, a moment's glance at a newsstand, a theater marquee, or a television program guide will instantly confirm. The medium has changed, but the popular Western lives on. To be sure, the message is neither so simple nor so reassuring as it once was. With the advance of the twentieth century have come cultural and worldwide dilemmas which have brought about significant alterations in the familiar formula: external conflicts are more commonly internalized; characters are more frequently morally ambivalent; plot situations are more complex and their resolutions more often equivocal. No longer a simple nobleman like Daniel Boone or Buffalo Bill, the Western hero of today is difficult to understand and classify. Often he is the dedicated professional of television's *Have Gun, Will Travel,* but he may also be the psychopathic killer of Sergio Leone's *For A Fistful of Dollars* or the living anachronism of *Butch Cassidy and the Sundance Kid.* He may even be the drunken buffoon of *Cat Ballou.* But though the formula has changed, vestiges of the standardized setting, stereotyped characters, and conventionalized plots that evolved in the dime novel are yet recognizable. In the saloons of Matt Dillon's Dodge City walk the shades of the bumbling sidekicks and tainted women who once stood beside Deadwood Dick in the boom towns of South Dakota. In television's *Grizzly Adams,* the buckskin-clad descendants of Daniel Boone still stare into the big sky, though with a more critical and worldly eye than did the patriarch of the wilds. So, too, western knights-errant rove the same rolling plains that Buffalo Bill roamed decades ago, though these days their guns are most often for hire. Altered, inverted, even parodied, the popular Western formula nonetheless survives. And it will continue to survive as long as it extends to humanity some glimmer of hope that a golden age still lies ahead.

VII. APPENDIX

i. NOTES

I. ORIGIN AND CONTEXT

[1]1(Dec. 1833), 578.

[2]Harold Arlo Blaine, "The Frontiersman in American Prose Fiction: 1800-1860," Diss. Western Reserve Univ. 1936, pp. 233, 246-247.

[3]*The Protective Policy in Literature: A Discourse on the Social and Moral Advantages of the Cultivation of Local Literature* (Columbus, Ohio: 1859), in Clarence Gohdes, "The Earliest Description of 'Western' Fiction?," *American Literature,* 37(Mar. 1965), 70-71.

[4]For the purposes of this study, I am defining the "Western" or "Western formula" as a mode of romance which is set somewhere along the moving frontier at a time when the values of wilderness and civilization are in tension, and which concerns the involvement of a highly stylized protagonist in some form of pursuit. This definition is meant to exclude stories which deal primarily with the agricultural West, and which might more accurately be termed "regional," "local color," or "realistic."

[5]A thorough history of the beginnings of the dime novel industry appears in Albert Johannsen, *The House of Beadle and Adams* (Norman: Univ. of Oklahoma Press, 1950), I, 3-6, 15-72. For a discussion of the standard formats and subject matter of the dime novel, see Russel B. Nye, *The Unembarrassed Muse: The Popular Arts in America* (New York: Dial, 1970), pp. 201-203.

[6]"Introduction," *Seth Jones by Edward S.*

Ellis and Deadwood Dick on Deck by Edward L. Wheeler: Dime Novels (New York: Odyssey, 1966), p. ix.

[7]Charles M. Harvey, "The Dime Novel in American Life," *Atlantic Monthly,* 100(July 1907), 40.

[8]"Critical Notices: Dime Books," *North American Review,* 24(July 1864), 303-304n.

[9]"Story Paper Literature," *Atlantic Monthly,* 54(Sept. 1879), 383.

[10]Merle Curti, "Dime Novels and the American Tradition," *Yale Review,* 26(Summer 1937), 761-778; Henry Nash Smith, *Virgin Land: The American West as Symbol and Myth* (1950; rpt. New York: Vintage-Knopf, n.d.); Kent Ladd Steckmesser, *The Western Hero in History and Legend* (Norman: Univ. of Oklahoma Press, 1965); Don Russell, *The Lives and Legends of Buffalo Bill* (Norman: Univ. of Oklahoma Press, 1960); and William A. Settle, Jr., *Jesse James Was His Name* (Columbia: Univ. of Missouri Press, 1966).

[11]Thoughout this study, my discussion of economic, social, moral, and legal trends during the nineteenth century is necessarily generalized. Statistics in this and subsequent paragraphs are taken from Allan Nevins and Henry Steele Commager, *A Pocket History of the United States,* 5th ed., rev. (New York: Washington Square Press, 1966), pp. 246-335. In-depth histories of the period are numerous, but especially enlightening are Douglas T. Miller, *The Birth of Modern America, 1820-1850* (New York: Western Publishing Co., 1970) and *Jacksonian Democracy: Class and Democracy in New York, 1830-1860* (New York: Oxford Univ. Press, 1967); Rowland Berthoff, *An Unsettled People: Social Order and Disorder in*

American History (New York: Harper & Row, 1971); and Perry Miller, *The Life of the Mind in America: From the Revolution to the Civil War* (New York: Harcourt, Brace, 1965).

[12]*Certain Dangerous Tendencies in American Life, and Other Papers* (Boston: n.p., 1880), pp. 167-168, in *Popular Culture and Industrialism,* ed. Henry Nash Smith (Garden City, N.Y.: Doubleday-Anchor, 1967), pp. 403-404.

[13]*Report on the Senate Committee on Education and Labor,* 2(1883), pp. 613-614, in Smith, *Popular Culture and Industrialism,* p. 404.

[14]Gelett Burgess, "The Confessions of a Dime Novelist," *Dime Novel Roundup,* No. 105(May 15,1941), 2.

[15]p. 5.

[16]"Dime Novel Days," *Dime Novel Roundup,* No. 112(Jan. 15, 1942), 2-3.

II. SETTING IN THE EARLY DIME NOVEL

[1]68(Jan. 1860), 33-36.

[2]p. 54.

[3]A number of full-length studies chart the impact upon the American psyche of the frontier and wilderness West. Among the best are Edwin Fussell, *Frontier: American Literature and the American West* (Princeton: Princeton Univ. Press, 1965); Lucy Lockwood Hazard, *The Frontier in American Literature* (1927; rpt. New York: Frederick Ungar Publishing Co., 1961); Leo Marx, *The Machine in the Garden: Technology and the Pastoral Ideal in America* (New York: Oxford Univ. Press, 1964); Roderick Nash, *Wilderness and the American Mind* (New Haven: Yale Univ. Press, 1967); Charles L. Sanford, *The Quest for*

Paradise: Europe and the American Moral Imagination (Urbana: Univ. of Illinois Press, 1961); and Henry Nash Smith, *Virgin Land: The American West as Symbol and Myth* (1950; rpt. New York: Vintage-Knopf, n.d.).

[4]*The Works of Orestes A. Brownson,* ed. Henry F. Brownson, 20 vols. (Detroit: 1882-1907), XV, 60, quoted in Nash, p. 94.

III. THE HERO IN TRANSITION

[1]G.H. Orians, "The Indian Hater in Early American Fiction," *Journal of American History,* 27, 1(1933), 33-44.

[2]My discussion of the Western hero's dialect, comic attributes, and rising social status is indebted to Henry Nash Smith's study of the Western hero in *Virgin Land: The American West as Symbol and Myth* (1950; rpt. New York: Vintage-Knopf, n.d.), a pioneer work from which no subsequent study of the dime novel can be wholly independent. I take exception, however, to Smith's overall conclusion that with the hero's replacement of "the genteel heroine as the pivotal center of plot construction, the Western story lost whatever chance it might once have had to develop social significance" (p. 134). To the contrary, the hero's replacement of the heroine "as the pivotal center of plot construction" was a refinement that permitted the narrative to carry out more efficiently its aesthetic and cultural functions.

[3]Smith, *Virgin Land,* pp. 90-98.

[4]Jay Monaghan, *The Great Rascal: The Life and Adventures of Ned Buntline* (New York: Bonanza Books, 1951), pp. 5-6.

[5]Colonel William F. Cody, *Life and Adventures of Buffalo Bill* (Chicago: Stanton and Van Vliet Co., 1917), pp. 265,267.

[6]Richard J. Walsh and Milton S. Salsbury, *The Making of Buffalo Bill* (Indianapolis: 1928), p. 221, in Joseph Schwartz, "The Wild West Show: 'Everything Genuine'," *Journal of Popular Culture,* 3(Spring 1970), 663.

[7]Frederic Remington, "Buffalo Bill in London," *Harper's Weekly,* 36 (Sept. 3, 1892), 847, in Schwartz, 662.

[8]Don Russell, *The Lives and Legends of Buffalo Bill* (Norman: Univ. of Oklahoma Press, 1960), pp. 387-388.

[9]J. Edward Leithead, "Buffalo Bill Item," *Dime Novel Roundup,* No. 61 (Apr. 15, 1937), 1-2.

[10]Russell, pp. 392-393.

[11]Albert Johannsen, *The House of Beadle and Adams* (Norman: Univ. of Oklahoma Press, 1950), II, 296.

[12]Though Deadwood Dick was a purely fictitious character, six men including Black cowboy Nat Love claimed the distinction of being the outlaw's real-life original. See Wayne Gard, "The Myth of Deadwood Dick," *Frontier Times,* 43 (Oct.-Nov. 1969), 10 ff.

[13]Ralph P. Smith, "Barred by the Post Office," *Dime Novel Roundup,* No. 145(Oct. 15, 1944), 1-5.

[14]William A. Settle, Jr., *Jesse James Was His Name* (Columbia: Univ. of Missouri Press, 1966), pp. 189-190.

[15]For a fuller discussion of the persecution and revenge motif in the Deadwood Dick stories, see my "Clenched Teeth and Curses: Revenge and the Dime Novel Outlaw Hero," *Journal of Popular Culture,* 7(Winter 1973), 652-665.

[16]The significance of this dime novel is also discussed by Kent Ladd Steckmesser, *The Western Hero in History and Legend* (Norman: Univ. of Oklahoma Press, 1965), pp. 73, 76.

[17]For another discussion of the dime novel cowboy's early popularizers, see Warren French, "The Cowboy in the Dime Novel," *Texas Studies in English,* 30(1951), 219-234.

[18]Joseph Waldmeir, "The Cowboy, the Knight, and Popular Taste," *Southern Folklore Quarterly,* 22(Sept. 1958), 116.

IV. SETTING IN THE LATER DIME NOVEL

[1]For an insightful discussion of the function of the standardized setting in the popular Western, see John G. Cawelti, *The Six-Gun Mystique* (Bowling Green, Ohio: Bowling Green Univ. Popular Press, 1971), pp.38-42 and *Adventure, Mystery and Romance: Formula Stories As Art And Popular Culture* (Chicago: University of Chicago Press, 1976), pp.192-259.

[2]p. 40.

[3]Quoted in Norman Foerster, *Nature in American Literature: Studies in the Modern View of Nature* (New York: Russell & Russell, 1958), p. 5.

V. STRUCTURE AND PLOT

[1]Northrop Frye, *Anatomy of Criticism: Four Essays* (1957; rpt. New York: Atheneum, 1970), pp. 186-187, 192-194.

[2]My discussion of the Western as a nineteenth century form of the *mythos* of romance is indebted to John G. Cawelti, *The Six-Gun Mystique* (Bowling Green, Ohio: Bowling Green Univ.

Popular Press, 1971), pp. 68-70.

[3]For a discussion of the evolution of the Indian captivity tale from a direct story of divine providence into a blood and thunder thriller, see Roy Harvey Pearce, "The Significance of the Captivity Narrative," *American Literature,* 19(1947), 1-20. The impact upon the dime novel of the plot and characters of the so-called "Indian plays" of nineteenth century melodrama is discussed in David Grimsted, *Melodrama Unveiled: American Theater and Culture, 1800-1850* (Chicago: Univ. of Chicago Press, 1968), pp. 215-220. Conversely, a discussion of the impact of the dime novel Western upon melodrama appears in Frank Rahill, *The World of Melodrama* (University Park: The Penn. State Univ. Press, 1967), pp. 235-238.

[4]Frye, pp. 195-197. Ethnological studies suggest that the pairing of symbolic, moral opposites is a characteristic element in the structure of all myths. The binary structure of primitive tribal myths, for example, has been demonstrated by Claude Levi-Strauss, *Mythologiques* (1966). With interesting results, Levi-Strauss' theories concerning the binary structure of myth have been adapted and applied to the popular Western film by Will Wright, *Six Guns and Society: A Structural Study of the Western* (Berkeley and Los Angeles: Univ. of California Press, 1975).

[5]Frye, p. 197.

[6]For a discussion of the relationship between sex and death in American fiction before 1860, see David Brion Davis, *Homicide in American Fiction, 1798-1860: A Study in Social Values* (Ithaca: Cornell Univ. Press, 1957), pp. 147-236.

[7]Douglas T. Miller, *The Birth of Modern America, 1820-1850* (New York: Western Publishing Co., 1970), p. 45.

[8]*The American Review: A Whig Journal of Politics, Literature, Art and Science,* 1(Jan. 1845), 95-98, in *The Nature of Jacksonian America,* ed. Douglas T. Miller (New York: John Wiley & Sons, 1972), p. 75.

[9]Miller, *The Birth of Modern America,* p. 103.

VI. THE UNIFYING VISION

[1]A discussion of the effect of rising second-class postal rates on the format of the dime novel appears in Ralph P. Smith, "Barred by the Post Office," *Dime Novel Roundup,* No. 145(Oct. 15, 1944), 1-5. In a personal letter to me dated May 24, 1971, Charles Bragin, noted dime novel collector and bibliographer, attributes the demise of the dime novel to the growing popularity of films.

ii. DIME NOVELS CITED (listed alphabetically by title)

A No. 1, the Dashing Toll-Taker; or, The Schoolmarm o' Sassafras. Edward L. Wheeler. Beadle's Half Dime Library, No. 299(Apr. 17, 1883).

Apollo Bill, the Trail Tornade; or, Rowdy Kate from Right-Bower. Edward L. Wheeler. Beadle's Half Dime Library, No. 236(Jan. 31, 1882).

Bear-Hunter; or, Davy Crockett as a Spy, The. Harry Hazard [Joseph E. Badger, Jr.]. Starr's American Novels, No. 118(May 27, 1873).

Big Foot Wallace, the King of the Lariat; or, Wild Wolf, the Waco. "Buckskin Sam" [Major Sam S. Hall]. Beadle's Dime Library, No. 204(Sept. 20, 1882).

Big George, the Giant of the Gulch; or, The Five Outlaw Brothers. Joseph E. Badger, Jr. Beadle's Dime Library, No. 88(Feb. 25, 1880).

Billy the Kid, the New Mexico Outlaw; or, The Bold Bandit of the West! Edmund Fable, Jr. Denver: Denver Publishing Co., 1881.

Black Hills Jezebel; or, Deadwood Dick's Ward, The. Edward L. Wheeler. Beadle's Half Dime Library, No. 201(May 31, 1881).

Boone, the Hunter; or, The Backwoods Belle. Frederick Whittaker. Beadle's Dime Novels, No. 278(Mar. 25, 1873).

Border Renegade; or, The Lily of the Silver Lake, The. Joseph E. Badger, Jr. Beadle's Dime Novels, No. 250(Feb. 27, 1872).

Boy Pards; or, Dainty Lance Unmasks, The. Joseph E. Badger, Jr. Beadle's Half Dime Library, No. 203(June 14, 1881).

Boy Rifle Rangers; or, Kit Carson's Three Young Scouts, The. "An Old Scout." Tousey's Pluck and Luck, No. 181(n.d.).

Buck Taylor, King of the Cowboys; or, The Raiders and the Rangers. Prentiss Ingraham. Beadle's Half Dime Library, No. 497(Feb. 1, 1887).

Buck Taylor, the Saddle King; or, The Lasso Rangers' League. Prentiss Ingraham. Beadle's Dime Library, No. 649(Apr. 1, 1891).

Buffalo Bill and His Merry Men; or, The Robin Hood Rivals. Prentiss Ingraham. Beadle's Dime Library, No. 735(Nov. 23, 1892).

Buffalo Bill in the Land of Fire; or, Nick Nomad, the Mountain Wanderer. "By the Author of Buffalo Bill." Original edition unidentified. Rpt. Street & Smith's Buffalo Bill Stories, No. 196 (1905?).

Buffalo Bill, the Buckskin King; or, The Amazon of the West. Major Dangerfield Burr [Prentiss Ingraham]. Beadle's Dime Library, No. 92(Apr. 21, 1880).

"Buffalo Bill, the King of the Border Men." Ned Buntline [Edward Zane Carroll Judson]. Street & Smith's *New York Weekly,* 25, Nos. 6-17(Dec. 23, 1869-Mar. 10, 1870).

Buffalo Bill's Blind Trail; or, Mustang Madge, the Daughter of the Regiment. Prentiss Ingraham. Beadle's Dime Library, No. 691(Jan. 20, 1892).

Buffalo Bill's Bonanza; or, The Knights of the Silver Circle. Prentiss Ingraham. Beadle's Dime Library, No. 644(Feb. 25, 1891).

Buffalo Bill's Double; or, The False Guide. "By the Author of Buffalo Bill" [Prentiss Ingraham?]. Original edition unidentified. Rpt. Street & Smith's Buffalo Bill Stories, No. 128(1903?).

Buffalo Bill's Featherweight; or, Apache Charley the Indian Athlete. "By the Author of Buffalo Bill" [Prentiss Ingraham]. Original edition unidentified. Rpt. Street & Smith's Buffalo Bill Stories, No. 145(1904?).

Buffalo Bill's Leap for Life: or, The White Death of Beaver Wash. "By the Author of Buffalo Bill." Original edition unidentified. Rpt. Street & Smith's Buffalo Bill Stories, No. 100(1902?).

Buffalo Bill's Queer Find; or, On a Lone Trail. Prentiss Ingraham. Original edition unidentified. Rpt. Street & Smith's Great Western Library, No. 74(1908).

Buffalo Bill's Spy Shadower; or, The Masked Man of Grand Canyon. Prentiss Ingraham. Beadle's Dime Library, No. 777(Sept. 13, 1893).

Cowboy Clan; or, The Tigress of Texas, The. Prentiss Ingraham. Beadle's Dime Library, No. 658(June 3, 1891).

Cowboy Steve, the Ranch Mascot; or, The Bond of Blood. William G. Patten. Beadle's Half Dime Library, No. 806(Jan. 3, 1893).

Dandy Dan of Deadwood and His Big Bonanza. "No name". Original edition of Tousey's Wide Awake Library unidentified. Rpt. New York: Gold Star Books Collector's Edition [IL7-37], n.d.

Daniel Boone, the Hero of Kentucky. Paul Braddon [William Howard Van Orden]. Tousey's Wide Awake Library, No. 152(n.d.). Rpt. Tousey's Wide Awake Library, No. 1186(Nov. 11, 1893).

Daniel Boone's Best Shot; or, The Perils of the Kentucky Pioneers. John Sherman. Original edition unidentified. Rpt. Tousey's Wide Awake Library, No. 1150(Dec. 3, 1892).

"Daredeath Dick, King of the Cowboys; or, In the Wild West with Buffalo Bill." Leon Lewis. Beadle's *Banner Weekly* (Nov. 6, 1886-Jan. 15, 1887). Rpt. Beadle's Dime Library, No. 629(Nov. 12, 1890).

Daring Davy, the Young Bear Killer; or, The Trail of the Border Wolf. Harry St. George [Harry St. George Rathborne]. Beadle's Half Dime Library, No. 108(Aug. 19, 1879).

Deadwood Dick of Deadwood; or, The Picked Party. Edward L. Wheeler. Beadle's Half Dime Library, No. 156(July 20, 1880).

Deadwood Dick on Deck; or, Calamity Jane, the Heroine of Whoop-Up. Edward L. Wheeler. Beadle's Half Dime Library, No. 73(Dec. 17, 1878).

Deadwood Dick, the Prince of the Road; or, The Black Rider of the Black Hills. Edward L. Wheeler. Beadle's Half Dime Library, No. 1(Oct. 15, 1877).

Deadwood Dick's Claim; or, The Fairy Face of Faro Flats. Edward L. Wheeler. Beadle's Half Dime Library, No. 362(July 1, 1884).

Deadwood Dick's Device; or, The Sign of the Double Cross. Edward L. Wheeler. Beadle's Half Dime Library, No. 104(July 22, 1879).

Forest Princess; or, The Kickapoo Captives, The. Joseph E. Badger, Jr. Beadle's Dime Novels, No. 227(Apr. 11, 1871).

Frontier Angel; or, A Romance of Kentucky Rangers' Life, The.

Edward S. Ellis. Beadle's Dime Novels, No. 15(Jan. 15, 1861).

Gunpowder Jim; or, The Mystery of Demon Hollow. J. Milton Hoffman. Original edition unidentified. Rpt. Beadle's Frontier Series, No. 37(1908).

Hunted Life; or, The Outcasts of the Border, The. Edward Willett. Beadle's Dime Novels, No. 125(June 4, 1867).

Hunter's Vow, The. Louis LeGrand [Mr. and Mrs. Victor?]. Beadle's Dime Novels, No. 66(Mar. 3, 1864).

Hurricane Hal, the Cowboy Hotspur; or, Old True Blue's Pilgrimage in Satan's Section. William G. Patten. Beadle's Dime Library, No. 676(Oct. 7, 1891).

Irona; or, Life on the Old South-West Border. Edward S. Ellis. Beadle's Dime Novels, No. 32(Nov. 23, 1861).

James Boys at Cracker Neck, The. D.W. Stevens. Original edition of Tousey's Wide Awake Library unidentified. Rpt. New York: Gold Star Books Collector's Edition [IL7-34], n.d.

James Boys in No Man's Land; or, The Bandit King's Last Ride, The. D. W. Stevens [John R. Musick?]. Tousey's New York Detective Library, No. 438(Apr. 18, 1891).

Joaquin, the Saddle King. A Romance of Murieta's First Fight. Joseph E. Badger, Jr. Beadle's Dime Library, No. 154(Oct. 5, 1881).

Joaquin, the Terrible. The True History of the Three Bitter Blows that Changed an Honest Man to a Merciless Demon. Joseph E. Badger, Jr. Beadle's Dime Library, No. 165(Dec. 21, 1881).

Kill-bar, the Guide; or, The Long Trail. Captain Comstock [Charles Dudley Warren?]. Starr's American Novels, No. 18(Feb. 1869).

Kiowa Charley, the White Mustanger; or, Rocky Mountain Kit's Last Scalp Hunt. Thomas Harbaugh. New York: Beadle and Adams, 1879.

Kit Carson, the Border Boy. C. Leon Meredith [George Blakelee]. Nickel Library Company's Little Chief Library, No. 184(n.d.).

Kit Carson, the Young Hunter. C. Leon Meredith [George

Blakelee]. Nickel Library Company's Little Chief Library, No. 185(n.d.).

Kit Carson's Bride; or, The Flower of the Apaches. George L. Aiken. Munro's Ten Cent Novels, No. 229(n.d.).

Lasso King's League; or, The Tigers of Texas, The. Prentiss Ingraham. Beadle's Dime Library, No. 653(Apr. 29, 1891).

"Mad Captain, The." Emerson Rodman. Street & Smith's *New York Weekly*(Nov. 1, 1866). Rpt. Boynton Belknap [pseud.].

Lew Wetzel, the Scout; or, The Captives of the Wilderness. Starr's American Novels, No. 16(1869).

Malaeska: The Indian Wife of the White Hunter. Ann S. Stephens. Beadle's Dime Novels, No. 1(June 9, 1860).

Man-Hunters; or, The Scourge of the Mines, The. Harry Hazard [Joseph E. Badger, Jr.]. Starr's American Novels, No. 60(Mar. 7, 1871).

Marshal of Satanstown; or, The League of the Cattle-Lifters, The. Frederick Whittaker. Beadle's Dime Library, No. 310(Oct. 1, 1884).

Mustang-Hunters; or, The Beautiful Amazon of the Hidden Valley, The. Frederick Whittaker. Beadle's Dime Novels, No. 226(Mar. 28, 1871).

Myrtle, the Child of the Prairie. Rose Kennedy. Beadle's Half Dime Novelettes, No. 1 (Dec. 5, 1860).

Nathan Todd; or, The Fate of the Sioux' Captive. Edward S. Ellis. Beadle's Dime Novels, No. 18(Mar. 1, 1861).

Old King Brady and 'Billy the Kid'; or, The Great Detective's Chase. Francis W. Doughty. Tousey's New York Detective Library, No. 411(Oct. 11, 1890).

Parson Jim, King of the Cowboys; or, The Gentle Shepherd's Big 'Clean Out'. Frederick Whittaker. Beadle's Dime Library, No. 215(Dec. 6, 1882).

Phantom Miner; or, Deadwood Dick's Bonanza, The. Edward L. Wheeler. Beadle's Half Dime Library, No. 42(May 14, 1878).

Pirate of the Placers; or, Joaquin's Death-Hunt, The. Joseph E. Badger, Jr. Beadle's Dime Library, No. 201(Aug. 30, 1882).

Queen of the Woods; or, The Shawnee Captive. "By the Author of 'The Silent Hunter' " [Percy St. John]. Beadle's Dime Novels, Nos. 152-155(June 9, 1868-July 24, 1868).

Quindaro; or, The Heroine of Fort Laramie. "By the Author of 'The Silver Bugle' " [Lieut. Col. Hazelton]. Beadle's Dime Novels, No. 77(Jan. 31, 1865).

"Red Arrow, the Wolf Demon; or, The Queen of the Kanawha." Albert Aiken. Beadle's *Saturday Journal,* I, Nos. 35-49(Nov. 12, 1870-Feb. 18, 1871). Rpt. *The Wolf Demon; or, The Queen of the Kanawha.* Beadle's Dime Library, No. 49(Aug. 21, 1878).

Red River Bill, the Prince of Scouts. J.R. Scott. Original edition unidentified. Rpt. Tousey's Wide Awake Library, No. 1311(Mar. 19, 1897).

Seth Jones; or, The Captives of the Frontier. Edward S. Ellis. Beadle's Dime Novels, No. 8(Oct. 2, 1860).

Sib Cone, the Mountain Trapper. Ned Buntline [Edward Zane Carroll Judson]. Starr's American Novels, No. 31(Jan. 11, 1870).

Silver-Mask, the Man of Mystery; or, The Cross of the Golden Keys. J.C. Cowdrick. Beadle's Half Dime Library, No. 360(June 17, 1884).

Solid Sam, the Boy Road-Agent; or, The Branded Brows. Edward L. Wheeler. Beadle's Half Dime Library, No. 141(Apr. 6, 1880).

Ted Strong's Nerve; or, Wild West Sport at Black Mountain. Ned Taylor [Harry St. George Rathborne]. Street & Smith's Young Rough Riders Weekly, No. 8(June 11, 1904).

Ted Strong's Rival; or, The Cowboys of Sunset Ranch. Ned Taylor [Harry St. George Rathborne]. Street & Smith's Young Rough Riders Weekly, No. 9(June 18, 1904).

Ted Strong's Rough Riders; or, The Boys of Black Mountain. Ned Taylor [Harry St. George Rathborne]. Street & Smith's Young Rough Riders Weekly, No. 1(Apr. 23, 1904).

Texan Trailer; or, Davy Crockett's Last Bear-Hunt, The. Chas. E. Lasalle [Edward S. Ellis]. Beadle's Dime Novels, No. 231(June 6, 1871).

Three-Fingered Jack, the Road-Agent of the Rockies; or, The Boy Miner of Hard Luck. Joseph E. Badger, Jr. Beadle's Dime Library, No. 28(Feb. 26, 1878).

Top Notch Tom, the Cowboy Outlaw; or, The Satanstown Election. Frederick Whittaker. Beadle's Dime Library, No.

303(Aug. 13, 1884).

True Life of Billy the Kid, The. Don Jenardo. Tousey's Wide
Awake Library, No. 451(Aug. 29, 1881).

Twin Scouts; A Story of the Old French War, The. W.J.
Hamilton. Beadle's Dime Novels, No. 92(Mar. 3, 1866).

"Viola Vennond; or, Life on the Border." Edward S. Ellis.
Philadelphia Dollar Newspaper, 20(July 2, 1862). Rpt.
Latham C. Carleton [pseud.]. *The Hunters; or, Life on the
Mountain and Prairie.* Irwin P. Beadle's Ten Cent Novels,
No. 1(Nov. 11, 1863). Rpt. Capt. J.F.C. Adams [pseud.].
The Fighting Trapper; or, Kit Carson to the Rescue.
Beadle's Dime Library, No. 68(May 21, 1879).

White Slayer, the Avenger; or, The Doomed Red-Skins. Maj.
Lewis W. Carson [Albert Aiken]. Starr's American
Novels, No. 37(Apr. 19, 1870).

*Wild Ivan, the Boy Claude Duval; or, The Brotherhood of
Death.* Edward L. Wheeler. Beadle's Half Dime Library,
No. 35(Mar. 26, 1878).

Wood King; or, Daniel Boone's Last Trail, The. Joseph E.
Badger, Jr. Beadle's Dime Novels, No. 288(Aug. 12, 1873).

iii. A SELECTED BIBLIOGRAPHY OF BOOKS AND ARTICLES CONCERNING DIME NOVELS AND STORY PAPERS

Bibliographies

There exists no single, comprehensive bibliography of
dime novels, but a number of shorter bibliographies are
helpful. The definitive bibliography of Beadle and Adams
publications is Albert Johannsen, *The House of Beadle and
Adams,* 2 vols. (Norman: Univ. of Oklahoma Press, 1950),
Supplement (1962). Volume II contains "A List of Some
Newspaper and Magazine Articles Dealing with Dime Novels,
Their Authors, and Dime-Novel Collectors" (1864-1950), and
the Supplement contains corrections and additions to this list.
Also helpful is Charles Bragin, *Bibliography: Dime Novels
1860-1964* (Brooklyn: Charles Bragin, 1964). A complete list of
Buffalo Bill dime novels appears in Don Russell, *The Lives and*

Legends of Buffalo Bill (Norman: Univ. of Oklahoma Press, 1960). *Dime Novel Roundup,* a monthly newsletter for collectors, publishes articles, notes, and occasional bibliographical listings.

Other References

Bishop, W.H. "Story Paper Literature." *Atlantic Monthly,* 54(Sept. 1879), 383-393.

Bluestone, George. "The Changing Cowboy: From Dime Novel to Dollar Film." *Western Humanities Review,* 14(Summer 1960), 331-337.

Branch, Douglas. *The Cowboy and His Interpreters.* 1926; rpt. New York: Cooper Square, 1961.

Cawelti, John G. *Adventure, Mystery, and Romance: Formula Stories as Art and Popular Culture.* Chicago: Univ. of Chicago Press, 1976.

_____. *The Six-Gun Mystique.* Bowling Green, Ohio: Bowling Green Univ. Popular Press, 1971.

Comstock, Anthony. *Traps For the Young.* Ed. Robert Bremner. 1883; rpt. Cambridge, Mass.: The Belknap Press of Harvard Univ., 1967.

Curti, Merle. "Dime Novels and the American Tradition." *Yale Review,* 26(Summer 1937), 761-778.

Durham, Philip. "Dime Novels: An American Heritage." *Western Humanities Review,* 9(Winter 1954-1955), 33-43.

_____. "Introduction," in *Seth Jones by Edward S. Ellis and Deadwood Dick on Deck by Edward L. Wheeler: Dime Novels.* New York: Odyssey Press, 1966, pp. v-xiii.

Dykes, J.C. "Dime Novel Texas; or, the Sub-Literature of the Lone Star State." *The Southwestern Historical Quarterly,* 49(Jan. 1946), 327-340.

Everett, William. "Critical Notices: Dime Books." *North American Review,* 24(July 1864), 303-309.

Foster, Thomas Henry. *Beadles, Bibles and Bibliophiles.* Cedar Rapids, Iowa: Torch Press, 1948.

French, Warren. "The Cowboy in the Dime Novel." *Texas Studies in English,* 30(1951), 219-234.

Gohdes, Clarence. "The Earliest Description of 'Western' Fiction?" *American Literature,* 37(Mar. 1965), 70-71.

Grimsted, David. *Melodrama Unveiled: American Theater and Culture, 1800-1850*. Chicago: Univ. of Chicago Press, 1968.

Harvey, Charles M. "The Dime Novel in American Life." *Atlantic Monthly,* 100(July 1907), 37-45.

Jones, Daryl E. "Blood n' Thunder: Virgins, Villains, and Violence in the Dime Novel Western." *Journal of Popular Culture,* 4(Fall 1970), 507-517.

_____ . "Clenched Teeth and Curses: Revenge and the Dime Novel Outlaw Hero." *Journal of Popular Culture,* 7(Winter 1973), 652-665.

Leithead, J. Edward. "The Saga of Young Wild West." *American Book Collector,* 19(March 1969), 17-22.

Monaghan, Jay. *The Great Rascal: The Life and Adventures of Ned Buntline*. New York: Bonanza Books, 1951.

Noel, Mary. "Dime Novels." *American Heritage,* 7 (Feb. 1956), 112-113.

_____ .*Villains Galore...the Heyday of the Popular Story Weekly*. New York: The Macmillan Company, 1954.

Nye, Russel B. *The Unembarrassed Muse: The Popular Arts in America*. New York: The Dial Press, 1970.

Pearson, Edmund. *Dime Novels; or, Following an Old Trail in Popular Literature*. Boston: Little, Brown, 1929.

Rahill, Frank. *The World of Melodrama*. University Park: The Penn. State Univ. Press, 1967.

Reynolds, Quentin. *The Fiction Factory: Or, From Pulp Row to Quality Street*. New York: Random House, 1955.

Russell, Don. *The Lives and Legends of Buffalo Bill*. Norman: Univ. of Oklahoma Press, 1960.

Settle, William A., Jr. "Literature as History: The Dime Novel as an Historian's Tool," in *Literature and History* (Univ. of Tulsa Monograph Series No. 9), ed. I.E. Cadenhead, Jr. Tulsa: Univ. of Tulsa, 1970, pp. 9-20.

_____ . *Jesse James Was His Name: or, Fact and Fiction Concerning the Careers of the Notorious James Brothers of Missouri*. Columbia: Univ. of Missouri Press, 1966.

Simmons, Michael K. "The Dime Novel and the American Mind." *Mankind,* 2(Oct. 1969), 58-63.

Smith, Henry Nash. "The Dime Novel Heroine." *Southwest Review,* 34(Spring 1949), 182-188.

_____. "The Western Hero in the Dime Novel." *Southwest Review,* 33(Summer 1948), 276-284.

_____. *Virgin Land: The American West as Symbol and Myth.* 1950; rpt. New York: Vintage-Knopf, n.d.

Steckmesser, Kent Ladd. *The Western Hero in History and Legend.* Norman: Univ. of Oklahoma Press, 1965.

Turner, E.S. *Boys Will Be Boys.* 2nd ed., rev., 1948; rpt. London: Joseph Michael Ltd., 1957.

Waldmeir, Joseph. "The Cowboy, The Knight, and Popular Taste." *Southern Folklore Quarterly,* 22(Sept. 1958), 113-120.